THE CRAFT OF
Cable-stitch
Knitting

BARBARA G. WALKER

Charles Scribner's Sons, New York

Glossary of Terms and Abbreviations

I. BASICS

K—Knit.

P—Purl.

St—Stitch. Sts—Stitches.

B—Work through the back loop of the stitch. "K1-b" means: knit one stitch through its back loop, inserting the needle into the stitch from the right-hand side. "P1-b" means: purl one stitch through its back loop, placing the right-hand needle point behind the stitch as if to insert the needle between the first and second stitches from the back, then inserting it, instead, into the *back* loop of the first stitch from the left-hand side, and wrapping the yarn around the needle point in front to complete the purl stitch as usual.

Sl—Slip. To pass a stitch or stitches from the left-hand needle to the right-hand needle without working them. The right-hand needle is always inserted into a stitch that is to be slipped *as if to purl* (i.e., from the right-hand side), unless directions specify "as if to knit" or "knitwise" (i.e., from the left-hand side).

Sl-st—Slip-stitch. A stitch that has been slipped.

Wyib—With yarn in back. Used with slip-stitches, it means that the yarn is carried across *behind* the stitch, on the side of the fabric that is *away from* the knitter. Whether this is a right or wrong side makes no difference.

Wyif—With yarn in front. When a stitch is slipped, the yarn is carried across in *front* of the stitch, on the side that is *facing* the knitter.

Rep—Repeat.

Rep from *—Repeat all material that comes after the *, in the same order.

( ) Parentheses—Indicates a repeat of material within the parentheses (or brackets) as many times as specified immediately after them; i.e., "(k2 tog, k1) 3 times" means: k2 tog, k1, k2 tog, k1, k2 tog, k1.

II. DECREASES

K2 tog—Knit two stitches together as one stitch.

P2 tog—Purl two stitches together as one stitch.

K2 tog-b—Insert the needle from the right into the back loops of two stitches at once, and knit them together as one stitch.

P2 tog-b—Turn the work over slightly and insert the needle from the left into the back loops of the second and first stitches, in that order, then wrap yarn around needle in front to complete the purl stitch. Same action as "p1-b" performed on two stitches at once. Note: In some circumstances, and for some knitters, "p2 tog-b" is awkward to work. The same effect can be obtained if desired by working the two stitches in the following manner: p1, sl the resulting st back to left-hand needle, then with point of right-hand needle lift the *next* stitch over the purled st and off the left-hand needle; then sl the same st back to right-hand needle and proceed. This is like a "psso" in reverse.

Sl 1, k1, psso—Slip 1 st wyib, knit 1 st, and pass the slipped stitch over; that is, insert the point of left-hand needle into the slipped stitch and draw it over the knit stitch and off the right-hand needle.

Ssk—Slip, slip, knit. This abbreviation is used almost always throughout this book, *instead of* the more usual "sl 1, k1, psso", because it is shorter, less easily confused with "sl 1, k2 tog, psso", and when done as directed makes a neater-looking decrease. Work "ssk" as follows: slip the first and second stitches *knitwise,* one at a time, then insert the tip of the left-hand needle into the *fronts* of these two stitches from the left, and knit them together from this position. (If, after trying this, the knitter still prefers to use "sl 1, k1, psso" for every "ssk", it is quite permissible to do so.)

Double decreases—These are k3 tog, p3 tog, k3 tog-b, sl 1—k2 tog—psso, all of which are self-explanatory; and p3 tog-b, which can be worked as described above under "p2 tog-b", by purling two stitches together, returning the resulting stitch to the left-hand needle, and passing the next stitch over. A double decrease makes 1 stitch out of 3.

NOTE: To work "k3 tog" so that it is the *exact opposite* of "sl 1—k2 tog—psso", do it this way: ssk, then sl the resulting st back to left-hand needle; then with point of right-hand needle pass the *next* stitch over the "ssk" stitch and off left-hand needle; then sl the st back to right-hand needle. This makes a double decrease slanting to the right, which will precisely match the left-slanting "sl 1—k2 tog—psso". It is a valuable trick especially for bisymmetrical lace patterns, where the decreases should always match.

Sl 2—k1—p2sso—This is a double decrease that is used when it is desirable to have the central stitch prominent. It is worked as follows: insert the needle into the fronts of the second and first stitches on the left-hand needle, as if to k2 tog; do not knit these stitches together, but *slip* them, both at once, from this position. Knit the next stitch on left-hand needle, then insert left-hand needle point into *both* slipped stitches at once and draw them *together* over the knit stitch and off right-hand needle, just as in "psso".

Sl 2—p1—p2sso—This double decrease is worked from the wrong side of the fabric, and is the corresponding opposite of "sl 2—k1—p2sso", likewise producing a dominant central stitch on the right side. Though it is not widely known, it should be in every knitter's repertoire of techniques because it is the only way to obtain this effect from the wrong side. Work "sl 2—p1—p2sso" as follows: turn the work over slightly, keeping yarn in front, and insert the needle from the left into the back loops of the second and first stitches, in that order, as if to p2 tog-b; do not purl these stitches together, but *slip* them, both at once, from this position. Purl the next stitch on left-hand needle, then insert left-hand needle point into *both* slipped stitches at once and draw them *together* over the purled stitch and off right-hand needle. The "p2sso" is just the same as when the decrease is worked from the right side.

III. INCREASES

Inc—Make two stitches out of one, by knitting into the front and back of the same stitch. This also may be done purlwise, by purling into the front and back of the same stitch, or it may be worked by (k1, p1) into one stitch, or (p1, k1) into one stitch.

4

M1—Make One. A method of adding a new stitch without leaving a hole or bump. Unless otherwise specified, it is done as follows: insert needle from behind under the *running thread* (which is the strand running from the base of the stitch just worked to the base of the next stitch) and lift this thread onto the left-hand needle; then knit one stitch into the *back* of it. "M1" can also be done purlwise, by purling into the back of the running thread, or by other methods which are explained in the patterns where they occur.

Knit next st in the row below—This is an increase *only* when followed by "then knit the st on needle". To knit in the row below, instead of working the loop that is *on* the needle, work into the loop that is immediately *under* the needle—i.e., the same loop that was on the needle in the preceding row. "Purl next st in the row below" is done the same way.

Yo—Yarn over. Take the yarn over the top of the needle once before making the next stitch. If the next stitch is to be knitted, then the yarn is simply taken over the top of the needle to the back, where it is in position to knit. If the next stitch is to be purled, then the yarn is taken over the needle to the back, then under the needle to the front, where it is in position to purl. (Note: English knitting directions distinguish between these by calling a yo before a knit switch "wf"—wool forward—and a yo before a purl stitch "wrn"—wool round needle.) A yo also may be worked in reverse: i.e., under the needle to the back, then over the needle to the front. This reverse yo is sometimes used on purl rows.

(Yo) twice, yo2, or 00—All these mean the same thing: a double yarn-over. The yarn passes over the needle to the back, under the needle to the front, and over the needle to the back again before making the next stitch, so that there are *two* extra strands on the needle. A double yarn-over is usually worked as two new stitches on the return row, by working (k1, p1) or (p1, k1) into the long loop.

(K1, yo, k1) in next st, (k1, p1, k1) in next st, (k1, yo, k1, yo, k1) in next st—these are various ways of making three or more stitches out of a single stitch. All material within the parentheses is to be worked in the *same* stitch before passing on to the next one.

IV. SPECIAL KNITTING ACTIONS

RT—Right Twist. K2 tog, leaving sts on left-hand needle; then insert right-hand needle from the front *between* the two sts just knitted together, and knit the first st again; then slip both sts from needle together. (For alternative method, see the introduction to chapter on Twist-Stitch Patterns.)

LT—Left Twist. With right-hand needle behind left-hand needle, skip one st and knit the second st in *back* loop; then insert right-hand needle into the backs of both sts (the skipped st and the second st) and k2 tog-b. (For alternative method, see the introduction to chapter on Twist-Stitch Patterns.)

FC—Front Cross. In cabling, the double-pointed needle carrying a stitch or stitches is held in *front* of the work (toward the knitter) while other stitches are being worked behind it. This produces a cable cross to the left.

BC—Back Cross. In cabling, the double-pointed needle carrying a stitch or stitches is held in *back* of the work (away from the knitter) while other stitches are being worked in front. This produces a cable cross to the right.

FKC, BKC, SFC, SBC, FPC, BPC, etc.—These are arbitrary abbreviations given with cable patterns when there are a number of different types of crossings in the same pattern, to distinguish one from another. Explanations are given in the individual pattern notes.

MB—Make Bobble. Usually done by increasing in one stitch, then working back and forth on the increased stitches for a specified number of short rows. Methods vary according to pattern.

V. GENERAL

Turn—This means that the work is turned around in the knitter's hands at some point *before* the end of a row, in order to work backward over the most recent stitches for a specified distance.

Short row—This is the knitting that is done after a turn. It may involve only a few stitches, or many—according to pattern—but in all cases the number of stitches in a short row is less than the total number of stitches on the needles.

Drop stitch—A stitch dropped off the needles. In some patterns it is picked up again after some other stitches have been worked; in other patterns it is unraveled downward for a certain number of rows and then picked up; in still other patterns it is simply left off the needles and ignored.

Dip stitch—A new stitch created by knitting into the fabric a certain number of rows below the stitches on the needle. The dip-stitch loop is drawn by the right-hand needle point through to the front and up, to be slipped on to the left-hand needle. Usually it is worked together with the next stitch on the needle.

Dpn—Double-pointed needle or cable needle.

Motif—The dominant figure or design unit in a pattern.

Panel—A portion of the knitting that develops a narrow vertical pattern, such as a cable, or an insertion in lace. For panel patterns directions are given in the number of stitches required to make the width of a single panel, rather than in multiples of stitches.

Spot-pattern or allover pattern—An arrangement of motifs all over the fabric, alternating at even intervals both vertically and horizontally.

Half-drop—A method of converting a panel pattern into a spot-pattern, by working the first half of the pattern rows in one panel along with the second half of the pattern rows in the adjoining panel.

MC—Main Color. The predominating color in a pattern of two or more colors.

CC—Contrasting Color. The "accent" color that is played against the main color.

Stockinette Stitch—"plain knitting". Knit right-side rows, purl wrong-side rows. For circular knitting, knit all rounds.

Reverse Stockinette Stitch—"purl fabric". Purl right-side rows, knit wrong-side rows. For circular knitting, purl all rounds.

Garter Stitch—knit all rows, both right and wrong sides. For circular knitting, knit one round, purl one round.

1

Cables

Not very many years ago, several kinds of sweaters peculiar to various coastal areas of the British Isles were suddenly discovered by the world of fashion. Their impact on that world was tremendous. Hardly ever before in history has any "peasant style" been so widely imitated, adapted, and adored. And hardly ever has so great an explosion of pattern ideas been derived from a single source.

For centuries, men and women in small fishing villages invented and developed prototypes of today's cable designs. Each family or clan had its own. When families were combined by intermarriage, family patterns also were combined into single garments. Combination of these patterns went on undisturbed for a long time, slowly developing a rich variety.

The Aran Isles, off the western coast of Ireland, are now famous as the source of the traditional fisherman sweater with its heavily embossed surface entirely covered by gorgeous cable combinations. But many other island and seaport localities contributed to the present abundance of cable designs. They come from Cornwall, Yorkshire, Guernsey, Jersey, and many other places. A special kind of fisherman sweater was known as the Bridal Shirt, traditionally knitted by the young fisherman or by his sweetheart, to be worn on his wedding day. The patterns in such garments were often inspired by things common to the daily work and life of the people: ropes, knots, chains, nets, waves, vines, berries, shellfish, driftwood.

It is a sad fact that when any particular branch of handicraft becomes wildly popular, it also becomes cheapened. In order to fill the world-wide demand for "Aran knits", knitwear manufacturers soon devised inexpensive ways to imitate them. Hand-knit sweaters, too, were made in hasty ways for the market, using bigger needles, fewer really intricate patterns, and hence less of the time and care necessitated by traditional methods.

But in the process of popularization, good things also happened to this type of knitting. Creative knitters everywhere began to build on the tradition, developing new and fascinating cable designs to be used along with the old ones. Therefore, many unusual contemporary cables will be found in this chapter, side by side with some of the classics. Today's hand knitter has no need to "make do" with the shoddy products that commercial fisherman sweaters all too often are. On the contrary, she can make cable-combination garments even more magnificent than the traditional ones, because she has more patterns to choose from than the old knitters ever had.

The great virtue of a cable-combination garment like a fisherman sweater is that it is—or should be—*one of a kind*. Cables can be put together according to the knitter's taste, and the result is something that no one else has ever done in just that way before. Anyone who has ever made *one* fisherman sweater will know how to make an original one by using different combinations. Patterns can be combined at will until the requisite number of stitches is achieved; then all that is necessary is to go ahead and knit them, keeping track of the row numbers in each one separately, so there is no confusion. Various panels can be packed closely together—the more the better—being set apart by no more than a single knit stitch. A rich profusion of embossed shapes is the mark of a truly fine Aran-style garment.

For the less ambitious knitter, there are many cables that can be worked all by themselves—just one or two panels—in an otherwise plain garment. Why leave a sleeve flat and unadorned, for instance, when an interesting cable panel can be run up the center of it? Why make a dull, plain cardigan for your husband, brother, father, son, or boy friend, when a pair of cables on each side of the front bands can make it look distinctively and handsomely masculine? It is so easy to designate the required number of stitches for your favorite cable, setting them off with markers if you like, and work the cable while the rest of the garment is being worked plain. It is a waste of your time and skill to hand-knit a garment all in stockinette stitch; a machine-made garment would serve just as well. Every garment you make should have a little bit of *you* in it, and this means a little bit of pattern that *you* have chosen for it. Cables are among the most adaptable patterns for this. They go anywhere, do anything, and always look in crisp, casual good taste.

It is curious, but true, that many people who have knitted for years have somehow managed to avoid trying their hands at even simple cables. This is a mistake, as some of the most interesting patterns in knitting are formed with the cable needle. The marvelous "fisherman sweaters" that are so popular today are made simply by combining different cable patterns in the same garment, and this is easier to do than you might think if you have never worked with cables. It is only a matter of keeping track of rows (the knitter's pencil-and-paper is one of the most essential parts of a fisherman sweater)! Even an otherwise plain garment is much improved, and acquires much more of the hand-knitted look, with the addition of a few cables. It really pays to become handy with the cable needle, and the technique, while a little awkward at first (like knitting itself, or any other skill) is soon mastered. Once it has been learned, the knitter can choose at will from a multitude of delightful combinations virtually without limit.

Nearly all cable patterns (with a few exceptions, like the all-over patterns of Basket Cable and Aran Honeycomb) are composed of knit stitches on a purl-stitch ground. When worked in a vertical direction, knit stitches tend to stand up away from purl stitches, giving an embossed effect. (In the horizontal direction, the opposite is true: purl stitches stand up in ridges against knit stitches.) Since most cables are used singly, the directions for them are given here in "panels", beginning and ending with the purl stitches on either side. (See Glossary on panels.)

In designing your own cable-stitch garments, or putting cable panels into a garment pattern which calls for plain stockinette, it is well to remember that cables tend to pull the fabric together laterally, so that more stitches are required to make the proper width. If you wish to insert a number of cable patterns into a sweater that is supposed to be done in plain knitting, it is a good idea to make it a size or two larger.

It is a very good habit to use a cable needle a size or two *smaller* than the needles being used for the rest of the work. This insures that the stitches will not be too much stretched while being cabled.

Cables (as well as other patterns) are sometimes worked in twisted stitches for a distinctive and different "corded" effect. This is not given with most of the following directions for various cables but you may try it out on any cable that you like, simply by knitting through the *back* loops of all the knit stitches on the right side that make up the cable, and purling through the *back* loops of the same stitches on the wrong side.

SPECIAL NOTE ON DESIGNING FISHERMAN SWEATERS

Everyone loves a fisherman sweater. How dazzling it is, heavily encrusted with fascinating embossed designs, the wonder and the envy of every inexperienced knitter! She can only admire it and think regretfully, "I could never make anything like that."

Nonsense. She can not only make it, she can even design it herself. Anyone who can use a cable needle can plan and work, not just any fisherman sweater, but an original fisherman sweater, using cable combinations that have never been put together in that particular way before. The result: a really unique garment, one of a kind, like no other sweater in the world. And it's actually very easy to do!

How to begin? All you need to start with is a number: the number of stitches required to reach halfway around the body of the person who will wear the sweater. This number is arrived at by taking the gauge of a cable swatch, or better yet the average of several different cable swatches, and multiplying by inches. For instance, let's say your own personal gauge on cable patterns, using a certain size needle and a certain yarn, is 6 stitches to the inch. Then, let's say you want your sweater to measure 20 inches across each of the front and back sections. 6 x 20 is 120 stitches; there's the number you need to start. An even easier (though rougher) way to get the number is to take it right from a commercial cable-sweater pattern. You simply look up the number of stitches given for a desired size, being sure that the gauge is the same as your own. If you are inexperienced, it is a good idea to continue following the same commercial pattern in regard to shaping the pieces as you go along. This eliminates the need for further measurements to establish when to begin decreases and so on.

All right, you have the number. Now comes the fun part. What patterns to use? There are dozens of traditional Aran patterns, all of them very beautiful, but you need not restrict yourself to these. Any cable or cable-stitch pattern is yours to create with. Leaf through this book and pick out half a dozen that you like. Other patterns not in the cable sections (such as Jacob's Ladder, Twist-Stitch Diamond Pattern, Trinity Stitch, Bobbles, etc.) are also traditionally used for fisherman sweaters but you need not stick to these either. So many hundreds of stunning

9

combinations are possible! The only thing that puts any limit at all to your choice is the matter of vertical gauge. For instance, slip-stitch patterns are usually unsuitable because they will require more rows than cables do for a given length. Of course all patterns that you consider using should be tried out first in test swatches.

Having selected some patterns that you would like to use, next take a piece of paper (graph paper is very good for this purpose) and mark off the panels of your sweater, beginning at the center. Let's say you have chosen a cable pattern of 20 stitches for your central panel. Mark 20 stitches, or 20 squares on the graph paper, for this panel. Next, on either side, you might mark another cable which happens to have a panel of 10 stitches, not forgetting to insert one knit stitch between panels to set them off. Now you have a center panel of 20 stitches, one knit stitch on either side, and two 10-stitch panels. 42 of your 120 stitches are used up. Add two more plain knit stitches on each side and continue building outward from the center in the same way, adding whatever patterns you like, until you have used almost all of the 120 stitches. Suppose you have five patterns all together—the center panel, which we will call A, Pattern B on each side of it, Pattern C next on each side, then two Pattern D's, and on the outside edges, two Pattern E's—each panel set off by single knit stitches between. At the end you have, say, 6 stitches left over on each side edge. These 12 edge stitches can be worked plain, or in any simple knit-purl texture pattern. The patterns most commonly used for this are Seed Stitch, Moss Stitch, and Double Seed Stitch.

Now you have established your patterns. You prepare to cast on for the back of your sweater. It is customary and desirable, when working any garment in cable patterns, to cast on fewer stitches for the ribbing and then increase to the desired number of stitches before beginning the cables themselves. This insures a better fit, as the cables will tighten the fabric above the ribbing. As a general rule you should cast on about 9 ribbing stitches for every 10 garment stitches. So you cast on 110 stitches, work in ribbing for as many inches as desired (twisted or fancy ribbing is preferable for fisherman sweaters), and then increase 10 stitches evenly spaced across the piece. You now have 120 stitches. On the next row set the patterns, following your diagram as you work across. To help out at the start, you can slip markers on the needle in between panels.

The best way to proceed, keeping track of which pattern row is being worked in each panel, is to write the names of the patterns (or A, B, C, D, and E) at the top of your paper and jot the number of each row under each pattern as you go along. Then, even though one pattern may have an 8-row repeat, another a 12-row repeat, and a third a 20-row repeat, you won't get them mixed up. It is very helpful sometimes to *know,* not just guess, that the row you are working on contains Row 9 of Pattern B and Row 13 of Pattern C and Row 3 of Pattern D. So do *not* try this sort of work without pencil and paper. If a mistake should be made, so that you have to unravel a few rows back to correct it, the written row count is an invaluable aid. It will tell you not only how many rows need to be taken out but also where to pick up each pattern when you begin again.

And there you are, launched on your own, unique, original fisherman sweater. The care and planning comes at the start. After the first repeat of the patterns has been worked, it's very easy indeed. Continue working just like a plain sweater, following a commercial pattern or using your own measurements for binding off and shaping above the underarm line. The sleeves are planned, set, and worked in the same way; and on the sleeves you can use those other different cables that you wanted to put in the body and didn't have room for—they need not match the body patterns.

When you are finished, you can be proud indeed. You will have a garment that is not only dazzling in its apparent complexity, but also totally *you*. You will have made your own individual creative contribution to the ancient art of knitting.

Simple Cables

Probably no pattern in knitting is capable of so much variation as the Simple Cable. But the cable action is always the same. It consists of taking half of the stitches composing the cable on a double-pointed needle, holding them in back or in front of the work, knitting the other half of the stitches, then knitting the first group from the double-pointed needle. This creates the cable twist. If the double-pointed needle with the slipped stitches is held in back of the work, the twist will be to the right (back cross); if the double-pointed needle is held in front of the work, the twist will be to the left (front cross). Whenever two Simple Cables are used on either side of a common center, one of them should be crossed in front and the other in back, to give symmetry and balance to the design.

The variations depend upon the number of stitches composing the cable, and the number of rows between cabling rows. Generally speaking, the most shapely cables are created by having the same number of rows to the pattern as there are stitches in the cable (i.e., a six-stitch cable would be crossed every 6th row, etc.) But this is hardly a firm rule. Many knitters prefer the slightly looser cable made with two more rows than there are stitches. And the number of rows may vary in the same pattern (See Eccentric Cable, below). Five possible variations on the Simple Cable are given, but there are dozens more. How you arrange a Simple Cable is largely up to you.

Simple Cables

LEFT TO RIGHT:
1. *Four-Stitch Cable crossed every 4th row.*
2. *Six-Stitch Cable crossed every 6th row.*
3. *Six-Stitch Cable crossed every 8th row.*
4. *Eccentric Cable*
5. *Eight-Stitch Cable crossed every 10th row.*

1. FOUR-STITCH CABLE CROSSED EVERY FOURTH ROW

Panel of 8 sts.

Rows 1 and 3 (Wrong side)—K2, p4, k2.
Row 2—P2, k4, p2.
Row 4—P2, sl next 2 sts to dpn and hold in back (or in front); k2, then k2 from dpn, p2.

Repeat Rows 1–4.

2. SIX-STITCH CABLE CROSSED EVERY SIXTH ROW

Six stitches is the most popular size for cables, though it is by no means necessary to stick to this number.

Panel of 10 sts.

Rows 1 and 3 (Wrong side)—K2, p6, k2.
Row 2—P2, k6, p2.
Row 4—P2, sl next 3 sts to dpn and hold in back (or in front); k3, then k3 from dpn, p2.
Row 5—As 1 and 3.
Row 6—As 2.

Repeat Rows 1–6.

3. SIX-STITCH CABLE CROSSED EVERY EIGHTH ROW

Panel of 10 sts.

Rows 1 and 3 (Wrong side)—K2, p6, k2.
Row 2—P2, k6, p2.
Row 4—P2, sl next 3 sts to dpn and hold in back (or in front); k3, then k3 from dpn, p2.
Rows 5 and 7—As 1 and 3.
Rows 6 and 8—As 2.

Repeat Rows 1–8.

4. ECCENTRIC CABLE

This is only one example of the many ways in which the pattern rows can be varied in the same cable. A long "wrapped-ribbon" effect can be had, for instance, by cabling only once in 20 or 30 rows. Or two cable rows may be placed close together and then three or four times as many rows worked plain in between. Once the principle is understood it can be applied at will.

Panel of 10 sts.

Rows 1 and 3 (Wrong side)—K2, p6, k2.
Row 2—P2, k6, p2.
Row 4—P2, sl next 3 sts to dpn and hold in back (or in front); k3, then k3 from dpn, p2.
Rows 5, 7, 9, 11, 13, 15, and 17—As 1 and 3.
Rows 6 and 8—As 2.
Row 10—As 4.
Rows 12, 14, 16, and 18—As 2.

Repeat Rows 1–18.

12

5. EIGHT-STITCH CABLE CROSSED EVERY TENTH ROW

This is a bulky, bold cable suitable for heavy sports sweaters and for coats.

Panel of 12 sts.

Rows 1 and 3 (Wrong side)—K2, p8, k2.
Row 2—P2, k8, p2.
Row 4—P2, sl next 4 sts to dpn and hold in back (or in front); k4, then k4 from dpn, p2.
Rows 5, 7, and 9—As 1 and 3.
Rows 6, 8, and 10—As 2.

Repeat Rows 1–10.

Double Cable or Horseshoe Cable

Just as in Simple Cables, many alterations in the appearance of a Double Cable may be made by varying the number of rows between cabling rows and the number of stitches composing the cable. The only limitation is that each cable must be made up of a number of stitches divisible by four, so that even crossings can be made on either side. There are two ways of cabling: (1) a back cross first and a front cross second, which opens the cable outward from the center; and (2) a front cross first and a back cross second, which closes the cable toward the center (Reverse Double Cable).

LEFT: *Double Cable or Horseshoe Cable*
CENTER: *Reverse Double Cable*
RIGHT: *Bulky Double Cable*

Panel of 12 sts.

Rows 1, 3, 5, and 7—(Wrong side)—K2, p8, k2.
Row 2—P2, sl next 2 sts to dpn and hold in back, k2, then k2 from dpn; sl next 2 sts to dpn and hold in front, k2, then k2 from dpn; p2.
Rows 4, 6, and 8—P2, k8, p2.

Repeat Rows 1–8.

REVERSE DOUBLE CABLE

Directions as above, except: read "hold in front" instead of "hold in back", and vice versa, in Row 2.

BULKY DOUBLE CABLE

Panel of 16 sts.

Rows 1, 3, 5, 7, and 9—(Wrong side)—K2, p12, k2.
Row 2—P2, sl next 3 sts to dpn and hold in back, k3, then k3 from dpn; sl next 3 sts to dpn and hold in front, k3, then k3 from dpn; p2.
Rows 4, 6, 8, and 10—P2, k12, p2.

Repeat Rows 1–10.

Wheat Ear Cable

This is a dense cable having the same basic structure as Double Cable, but with the cabling rows closer together and one additional stitch in the center. The same Wheat Ear pattern may be worked on a panel of 13 sts, with a 9-stitch cable (reading "2" for "3" in Row 3.)

Panel of 17 sts.

Row 1 (Right side)—P2, k13, p2.
Row 2—K2, p13, k2.
Row 3—P2, sl next 3 to dpn and hold in back, k3, k3 from dpn, k1, sl next 3 to dpn and hold in front, k3, k3 from dpn, p2.
Row 4—K2, p13, k2.

Repeat Rows 1–4.

VARIATION: *REVERSE WHEAT EAR CABLE*

Work the same as Wheat Ear Cable, except exchange the words "back" and "front" in Row 3. This variation is useful for making a classic Wheat Ear in a garment worked from the top down; or it may be done in reverse fashion from the bottom up if the knitter prefers.

LEFT: *Wheat Ear Cable*
RIGHT: *Reverse Wheat Ear Cable*

Plait Cable

This type of cable is a little more sophisticated than a Simple Cable, but just as easy to work.

Panel of 13 sts.

Row 1 (Right side)—P2, k9, p2.
Row 2—K2, p9, k2.
Row 3—P2, sl next 3 sts to dpn and hold in front, k3, then k3 from dpn; k3, p2.
Rows 4 and 6—As Row 2.
Row 5—As Row 1.
Row 7—P2, k3, sl next 3 sts to dpn and hold in back, k3, then k3 from dpn; p2.
Row 8—As Row 2.

Repeat Rows 1–8.

VARIATION

If a *back* cross is worked in Row 3 (i.e., "hold in back" instead of "hold in front") and a *front* cross in Row 7 (i.e., "hold in

LEFT: *Plait Cable*
CENTER: *Little Plait Cable*
RIGHT: *Reverse Plait Cable or Branch Cable*

front" instead of "hold in back"), all other directions remaining the same, the pattern is reversed. This Reverse Plait is sometimes known as Branch Cable.

LITTLE PLAIT CABLE

Panel of 10 sts.

Rows 1 and 3 (Wrong side)—K2, p6, k2.
Row 2—P2, sl next 2 sts to dpn and hold in front, k2, then k2 from dpn; k2, p2.
Row 4—P2, k2, sl next 2 sts to dpn and hold in back, k2, then k2 from dpn; p2.

Repeat Rows 1–4.

Wave Cable or Ribbon Stitch

Instead of being twisted in the usual way, the cabled stitches here are moved back and forth to form an embossed wave. Wave Cable is a popular Aran pattern, often used—along with its relative, the Chain Cable—in fisherman sweaters. When two Wave Cables are worked, one on either side of a common center, then one of the cables should be started with Row 1 and the other with Row 7, so that the "waves" will balance each other.

Panel of 10 sts.

Row 1 (Wrong side) and all other wrong-side rows—K2, p6, k2.
Row 2—P2, sl next 3 sts to dpn and hold in back, k3, then k3 from dpn; p2.
Rows 4 and 6—P2, k6, p2.
Row 8—P2, sl next 3 sts to dpn and hold in front, k3, then k3 from dpn; p2.
Rows 10 and 12—P2, k6, p2.

Repeat Rows 1–12.

LEFT TO RIGHT:
1. *Wave Cable or Ribbon Stitch*
2. *Elongated Wave Cable*
3. *Chain Cable or Double Ribbon Stitch*
4. *Elongated Chain Cable*

VARIATION: ELONGATED WAVE CABLE

There are a number of ways of varying a Wave Cable, both in the number of stitches and the number of rows. This Elongated Wave Cable shows one method of variation.

Panel of 8 sts.

Row 1 (Wrong side) and all other wrong-side rows—K2, p4, k2.
Row 2—P2, sl next 2 sts to dpn and hold in back, k2, then k2 from dpn; p2.
Rows 4, 6, and 8—P2, k4, p2.
Row 10—P2, sl next 2 sts to dpn and hold in front, k2, then k2 from dpn; p2.
Rows 12, 14, and 16—P2, k4, p2.

Repeat Rows 1–16.

15

Chain Cable or Double Ribbon Stitch

(*See illustration, page 15*)

This famous cable is the basis of the Aran Honeycomb, which is essentially a number of Chain Cables worked side by side, and in contact with each other, across the entire fabric.

Panel of 12 sts.

Row 1 (Wrong side) and all other wrong-side rows—K2, p8, k2.

Row 2—P2, sl next 2 sts to dpn and hold in back, k2, then k2 from dpn; sl next 2 sts to dpn and hold in front, k2, then k2 from dpn; p2.

Row 4—P2, k8, p2.

Row 6—P2, sl next 2 sts to dpn and hold in front, k2, then k2 from dpn; sl next 2 sts to dpn and hold in back, k2, then k2 from dpn; p2.

Row 8—P2, k8, p2.

Repeat Rows 1–8.

VARIATION: *ELONGATED CHAIN CABLE*

In this version the Chain Cable is elongated by only two more rows inserted between cabling rows. Four more could be used also. The Elongated Wave Cable verges on the Medallion Cable, which has a similar form but somewhat larger proportions.

Panel of 12 sts.

Row 1 (Wrong side) and all other wrong-side rows—K2, p8, k2.

Row 2—P2, sl next 2 sts to dpn and hold in back, k2, then k2 from dpn; sl next 2 sts to dpn and hold in front, k2, then k2 from dpn; p2.

Rows 4 and 6—P2, k8, p2.

Row 8—P2, sl next 2 sts to dpn and hold in front, k2, then k2 from dpn; sl next 2 sts to dpn and hold in back, k2, then k2 from dpn; p2.

Rows 10 and 12—P2, k8, p2.

Repeat Rows 1–12.

Medallion Cable

This is similar to the Chain Cable, except that it has one additional stitch in the center and more rows between cable rows. The Medallion Cable lends itself readily to extra ornamentation in the center of the "medallion", for instance with a Bobble formed in the center stitch at each repetition of Row 1.

Panel of 17 sts.

Rows 1 and 3 (Right side)—P2, k13, p2.

Rows 2 and 4—K2, p13, k2.

Row 5—P2, sl next 3 to dpn and hold in front, k3, k3 from dpn,
    k1, sl next 3 to dpn and hold in back, k3, k3 from dpn, p2.
Rows 6, 8, and 10—K2, p13, k2.
Rows 7, 9, and 11—P2, k13, p2.
Row 12—K2, p13, k2.
Row 13—P2, sl next 3 to dpn and hold in back, k3, k3 from
    dpn, k1, sl next 3 to dpn and hold in front, k3, k3 from
    dpn, p2.
Row 14—K2, p13, k2.
Row 15—P2, k13, p2.
Row 16—K2, p13, k2.

Repeat Rows 1–16.

LEFT: *Medallion Cable*
CENTER: *Tyrolean Medallion*
RIGHT: *Round Cable*

Tyrolean Medallion

The large round medallion traditionally is ornamented with
bobbles or embroidered flowers, or both.

Panel of 19 sts.

Row 1 (Wrong side)—K2, p15-b, k2.
Row 2—P2, sl next 3 sts to dpn and hold in front, k3-b, then k3-b from dpn; k3-b,
    sl next 3 sts to dpn and hold in back, k3-b, then k3-b from dpn; p2.
Rows 3 and 5—K2, p15-b, k2.
Rows 4 and 6—P2, k15-b, p2.
Row 7—K2, p15-b, k2.
Row 8—P2, sl next 3 sts to dpn and hold in back, k3-b, then k3-b from dpn;
    k3-b, sl next 3 sts to dpn and hold in front, k3-b, then k3-b from dpn; p2.
Rows 9–16—Repeat Rows 3 through 6 twice.

Repeat Rows 1–16.

Round Cable

Panel of 12 sts.

Rows 1, 3, and 5 (Wrong side)—K4, p4, k4.
Rows 2 and 4—P4, k4, p4.
Row 6—P2, sl next 2 sts to dpn and hold in back, k2, then p2 from dpn; sl next
    2 sts to dpn and hold in front, p2, then k2 from dpn; p2.
Rows 7, 9, and 11—K2, p2, k4, p2, k2.
Rows 8 and 10—P2, k2, p4, k2, p2.
Row 12—P2, sl next 2 sts to dpn and hold in front, p2, then k2 from dpn; sl next
    2 sts to dpn and hold in back, k2, then p2 from dpn; p2.

Repeat Rows 1–12.

17

Gull Stitch

Sometimes known as Wishbone Cable, this is a very beautiful old pattern often seen in Aran sweaters.

Panel of 10 sts.

Row 1 (Wrong side)—K2, p6, k2.
Row 2—P2, k2, sl 2 wyib, k2, p2.
Row 3—K2, p2, sl 2 wyif, p2, k2.
Row 4—P2, sl next 2 sts to dpn and hold in back, k1, then k2 from dpn; sl next st to dpn and hold in front, k2, then k1 from dpn; p2.

Repeat Rows 1–4.

Triple Gull-Stitch Cable

Panel of 10 sts.

Row 1 (Right side)—P2, k6, p2.
Row 2—K2, p6, k2.
Row 3—P2, k6, p2.
Row 4—K2, p2, sl 2 wyif, p2, k2.
Row 5—P2, sl next 2 to dpn and hold in back, k1, k2 from dpn; sl next st to dpn and hold in front, k2, k the st from dpn, p2.
Rows 6–9—Repeat Rows 4 and 5 twice more.
Row 10—K2, p6, k2.
Row 11—P2, k6, p2.
Row 12—K2, p6, k2.

Repeat Rows 1–12.

Inverted Gull Stitch

This cable is not a true Gull Stitch because the stitches are not slipped before being cabled. However, it does resemble a Gull Stitch widened and turned upside down. Note that there is an extra stitch in the center, as in Wheat Ear Cable.

Panel of 13 sts.

Rows 1 and 3 (Wrong side)—K2, p9, k2.
Row 2—P2, sl next st to dpn and hold in front, k3, then k1 from dpn; k1, sl next 3 sts to dpn and hold in back, k1, then k3 from dpn; p2.
Row 4—P2, k9, p2.

Repeat Rows 1–4.

LEFT: *Gull Stitch*
CENTER: *Triple Gull-Stitch Cable*
RIGHT: *Inverted Gull Stitch*

Braid Cables

Braid Cables (not to be confused with Plait Cables) consist of three knit ribs traveling across a purl-stitch ground, and crossing one another alternately in true braid fashion. Braid Cables are novel in appearance and interesting to work. Also, they are capable of much variation. Three types of Braid Cable are given: Close, Barred, and Twisted. Other variations, of course, are possible.

LEFT: *Close Braid Cable*
CENTER: *Barred Braid Cable*
RIGHT: *Twisted Braid Cable*

CLOSE BRAID CABLE

Panel of 13 sts.

NOTE: Front Cross (FC)—sl 2 sts to dpn and hold in front, p1, then k2 from dpn. Back Cross (BC)—sl 1 st to dpn and hold in back, k2, then p1 from dpn.

Row 1 (Wrong side)—K3, p4, k2, p2, k2.
Row 2—P2, FC, BC, FC, P2.
Row 3 and all subsequent wrong-side rows—Knit all knit sts and purl all purl sts.
Row 4—P3, sl next 2 sts to dpn and hold in back, k2, then k2 from dpn; p2, k2, p2.
Row 6—P2, BC, FC, BC, p2.
Row 8—P2, k2, p2, sl next 2 sts to dpn and hold in front, k2, then k2 from dpn; p3.

Repeat Rows 1–8.

BARRED BRAID CABLE

Panel of 16 sts.

NOTE: FC and BC—same as for Close Braid Cable.

Row 1 (Right side)—P2, FC, p2, BC, FC, p3.
Row 2—K3, (yo, p2, pass yo over 2 purled sts, k2) 3 times, k1.
Row 3—P3, FC, BC, p2, FC, p2.
Row 4—K2, yo, p2, pass yo over 2 purled sts, k4, (yo, p2, pass yo over 2 purled sts) twice, k4.
Row 5—P4, sl next 2 sts to dpn and hold in back, k2, then k2 from dpn; p4, k2, p2.
Row 6—As Row 4.
Row 7—P3, BC, FC, p2, BC, p2.
Row 8—As Row 2.
Row 9—P2, BC, p2, FC, BC, p3.
Row 10—K4, (yo, p2, pass yo over 2 purled sts) twice, k4, yo, p2, pass yo over 2 purled sts, k2.
Row 11—P2, k2, p4, sl next 2 sts to dpn and hold in front, k2, then k2 from dpn; p4.
Row 12—As Row 10.

Repeat Rows 1–12.

TWISTED BRAID CABLE

Panel of 11 sts.

NOTE: Front Cross (FC)—sl 1 st to dpn and hold in front, p1, then k1-b from dpn. Back Cross (BC)—sl 1 st to dpn and hold in back, k1-b, then p1 from dpn.

Row 1 (Wrong side)—K3, p2-b, k4, p1-b, k1.
Row 2—P1, FC, p2, BC, FC, p2.
Row 3 and all subsequent wrong-side rows—K all knit sts and p-b all purl sts.
Row 4—P2, FC, BC, p2, FC, p1.
Row 6—P3, sl next st to dpn and hold in back, k1-b, then k1-b from dpn; p4, k1-b, p1.
Row 8—P2, BC, FC, p2, BC, p1.
Row 10—P1, BC, p2, FC, BC, p2.
Row 12—P1, k1-b, p4, sl next st to dpn and hold in front, k1-b, then k1-b from dpn; p3.

Repeat Rows 1–12.

CENTER PANEL: *Tree of Life*
SIDE PANELS: *Twisted Tree*

Tree of Life

This is a famous old Aran pattern.

Panel of 15 sts.

Row 1 (Right side)—P2, k1, p4, sl 1 wyib, p4, k1, p2.
Row 2—K2, sl 1 wyif, k4, p1, k4, sl 1 wyif, k2.
Row 3—P2, sl 1 to dpn and hold in front, p1; k1 from dpn (Front Cross or FC); p3, sl 1 wyib, p3; sl 1 to dpn and hold in back, k1; p1 from dpn (Back Cross or BC); p2.
Row 4—K3, sl 1 wyif, k3, p1, k3, sl 1 wyif, k3.
Row 5—P3, FC, p2, sl 1 wyib, p2, BC, p3.
Row 6—K4, sl 1 wyif, k2, p1, k2, sl 1 wyif, k4.
Row 7—P4, FC, p1, sl 1 wyib, p1, BC, p4.
Row 8—K5, sl 1 wyif, k1, p1, k1, sl 1 wyif, k5.
Row 9—P2, k1, p2, FC, sl 1 wyib, BC, p2, k1, p2.
Row 10—K2, sl 1 wyif, k4, p1, k4, sl 1 wyif, k2.

On subsequent repeats omit Rows 1 and 2 and repeat Rows 3–10.

Twisted Tree

This is a variant on the Tree of Life theme, but in reverse; the Twisted Tree does not droop but rather opens its "branches" upward. Note also the contrast between the large loose slip-stitches of the classic Tree of Life, and the tightly twisted stitches in this pattern.

Panel of 9 sts.

Row 1 (Right side)—P3, k3-b, p3.
Row 2—K3, p3-b, k3.
Row 3—P2, sl next st to dpn and hold in back, k1-b, then p1 from dpn (Back Cross, BC); k1-b, sl next st to dpn and hold in front, p1, then k1-b from dpn (Front Cross, FC); p2.
Row 4—K2, (p1-b, k1) twice, p1-b, k2.
Row 5—P1, BC, p1, k1-b, p1, FC, p1.
Row 6—K1, (p1-b, k2) twice, p1-b, k1.
Row 7—BC, p1, k3-b, p1, FC.
Row 8—P1-b, k2, p3-b, k2, p1-b.

Repeat Rows 1–8.

Staghorn Cable

This is a graceful, easy pattern for any spot where a wide cable is needed. The method of doing it in reverse is handy for a Staghorn effect in any garment that is knitted from the top down. Also, the Reverse Staghorn is a pretty cable in its own right. Staghorn and Reverse Staghorn are attractive when used together in alternate panels.

LEFT: *Staghorn Cable*
RIGHT: *Reverse Staghorn Cable*

Panel of 20 sts.

NOTE: Back Cross (BC)—sl 2 sts to dpn and hold in back, k2, then k2 from dpn. Front Cross (FC)—sl 2 sts to dpn and hold in front, k2, then k2 from dpn.

Rows 1, 3, and 5 (Wrong side)—K2, p16, k2.
Row 2—P2, k4, BC, FC, k4, p2.
Row 4—P2, k2, BC, k4, FC, k2, p2.
Row 6—P2, BC, k8, FC, p2.

Repeat Rows 1–6.

REVERSE STAGHORN CABLE

Panel of 20 sts.

NOTE: BC and FC—as above.

Rows 1, 3, and 5 (Wrong side)—K2, p16, k2.
Row 2—P2, FC, k8, BC, p2.
Row 4—P2, k2, FC, k4, BC, k2, p2.
Row 6—P2, k4, FC, BC, k4, p2.

Repeat Rows 1–6.

Triple-Braided Diamonds

This is a fascinating pattern of large diamonds intricately braided together, ideal for a central panel in a fancy sweater.

CENTER PANEL: *Triple-Braided Diamonds*
SIDE PANELS: *Wave of Honey Cable or Little Chain*

Panel of 30 sts.

NOTES: Front Cross or FC—sl 2 k sts to dpn and hold in front, p1, then k2 from dpn.

Back Cross or BC—sl 1 p st to dpn and hold in back, k2, then p the st from dpn.

Front Double Knit Cross or FDKC—sl 2 k sts to dpn and hold in front, k2, then k2 from dpn.

Back Double Knit Cross or BDKC—sl 2 k sts to dpn and hold in back, k2, then k2 from dpn.

Row 1 (Wrong side)—K7, (p4, k2) twice, p4, k7.

Row 2—P6, (BC, FC) 3 times, p6.

Row 3 and all other wrong-side rows—Knit all knit sts and purl all purl sts.

Row 4—P5, BC, (p2, BDKC) twice, p2, FC, p5.

Row 6—P4, BC, p2, (BC, FC) twice, p2, FC, p4.

Row 8—P3, (BC, p2) twice, FDKC, (p2, FC) twice, p3.

Row 10—(P2, BC) 3 times, (FC, p2) 3 times.

Row 12—Knit all k sts and purl all p sts.

Row 14—(P2, FC) 3 times, (BC, p2) 3 times.

Row 16—P3, (FC, p2) twice, FDKC, (p2, BC) twice, p3.

Row 18—P4, FC, p2, (FC, BC) twice, p2, BC, p4.

Row 20—P5, FC, (p2, BDKC) twice, p2, BC, p5.

Row 22—P6, (FC, BC) 3 times, p6.

Row 24—P7, (FDKC, p2) twice, FDKC, p7.

Repeat Rows 1–24.

Wave of Honey Cable or Little Chain

This beautiful little cable is the designing unit of Wave of Honey Stitch (which see). It is very decorative and has many uses. Try, for instance, a continuous row of Wave of Honey Cables, with two purl stitches between, for a fancy ribbing.

Panel of 8 sts.

Rows 1 and 3 (Wrong side)—K2, p4, k2.

Row 2—P2, sl next st to dpn and hold in front, k1, then k1 from dpn; sl next st to dpn and hold in back, k1, then k1 from dpn; p2.

Row 4—P2, sl next st to dpn and hold in back, k1, then k1 from dpn; sl next st to dpn and hold in front, k1, then k1 from dpn; p2.

Repeat Rows 1–4.

Valentine Cable

A hand-knitted gift sweater is surely a labor of love, and all the more evidently so when it carries this handsome heart-shaped pattern. Note that the first 3 rows are preparatory, not to be repeated after the pattern has been started.

CENTER PANEL: *Valentine Cable*
SIDE PANELS: *Ribbed Cable*

Panel of 16 sts.

Rows 1 and 3 (Wrong side)—K6, p4, k6.

Row 2—P6, sl next 2 sts to dpn and hold in front, k2, then k2 from dpn; p6.

Row 4—P5, sl next st to dpn and hold in back, k2, then p1 from dpn (Back Cross, BC); sl next 2 sts to dpn and hold in front, p1, then k2 from dpn (Front Cross, FC); p5.

Row 5—K5, p2, k2, p2, k5.

Row 6—P4, BC, p2, FC, p4.

Row 7—(K4, p2) twice, k4.

Row 8—P3, BC, p4, FC, p3.

Row 9—K3, p2, k6, p2, k3.

Row 10—P2, (BC) twice, (FC) twice, p2.

Row 11—K2, (p2, k1, p2, k2) twice.

Row 12—P1, (BC) twice, p2, (FC) twice, p1.

Row 13—(K1, p2) twice, k4, (p2, k1) twice.

Row 14—P1, k1, sl 1 st to dpn and hold in front, p1, then k1 from dpn (Single FC); FC, p2, BC, sl 1 st to dpn and hold in back, k1, then p1 from dpn (Single BC); k1, p1.

Row 15—(K1, p1) twice, k1, p2, k2, p2, k1, (p1, k1) twice.

Row 16—P1, k1, p1, Single FC. FC, BC, Single BC, p1, k1, p1.

Row 17—K1, p1, k2, p1, k1, p4, k1, p1, k2, p1, k1.

Row 18—P1, Single FC, Single BC, p1, sl next 2 sts to dpn and hold in front, k2, then k2 from dpn; p1, Single FC, Single BC, p1.

Row 19—K2, sl next st to dpn and hold in back, k1, then k1 from dpn; k2, p4, k2, sl next st to dpn and hold in front, k1, then k1 from dpn; k2.

Omit Rows 1 through 3, repeat Rows 4–19.

Ribbed Cable

The Ribbed Cable is very elegant, and is frequently seen in fisherman sweaters. Note that there are two ways of working Row 2, and that in both cases the knit stitches are purled and the purl stitches knitted in the 4-stitch group. When two Ribbed Cables are used on either side of a common center, one should be done by the front-cross method and the other by the back-cross method, to balance the patterns. For a Ribbed Wave Cable, work the front-cross and back-cross methods alternately, every 10th row in the same cable.

Panel of 11 sts.

Row 1 (Wrong side)—K2, (p1-b, k1) 3 times, p1-b, k2.

Row 2—For a front-cross cable work Row 2 as follows: P2, sl next 3 sts to dpn and hold in front, (k1-b, p1) twice on next 4 sts, then from dpn k1-b, p1, k1-b the 3 sts, p2.

For a back-cross cable work Row 2 as follows: P2, sl next 4 sts to dpn and hold in back, k1-b, p1, k1-b on next 3 sts, then from dpn (p1, k1-b) twice, p2.

Rows 3, 5, 7, and 9—As Row 1.

Rows 4, 6, 8, and 10—P2, (k1-b, p1) 3 times, k1-b, p2.

Repeat Rows 1–10.

Superimposed Double Wave

CENTER PANEL: *Superimposed Double Wave*
SIDE PANELS: *Oxox Cable*

This is a beautiful pattern of four separated waves interpenetrating each other, two on top and two beneath. Very good for fancy sweaters.

Panel of 16 sts.

NOTES: Front Cross or FC—sl 2 k sts to dpn and hold in front, p1, then k2 from dpn. Back Cross or BC—sl 1 p st to dpn and hold in back, k2, then p the st from dpn. Front Double Knit Cross or FDKC—sl 2 k sts to dpn and hold in front, k2, then k2 from dpn.

Row 1 (Right side)—K2, p3, k2, p2, k2, p3, k2.

Row 2—and all other wrong-side rows—Knit all k sts and purl all p sts.

Row 3—FC, p2, FC, BC, p2, BC.

Row 5—P1, FC, p2, FDKC, p2, BC, p1.

Row 7—P2, (FC, BC) twice, p2.

Row 9—P3, FDKC, p2, FDKC, p3.

Row 11—P2, (BC, FC) twice, p2.

Row 13—P1, BC, p2, FDKC, p2, FC, p1.

Row 15—BC, p2, BC, FC, p2, FC.

Row 16—See Row 2.

Rows 17 through 32—work exactly as Rows 1–16 *except* in Rows 5, 9, and 13 substitute *Back* Double Knit Cross for FDKC. This is worked as FDKC but hold the sts in back instead of in front.

Repeat Rows 1–32.

NOTE: If Rows 1–16 *only* are repeated, then the cable will be twisted in the usual cable fashion, instead of being superimposed.

Oxox Cable

This curiously named cable is a variation on Chain Cable. Its name describes it: the "chain" cabling action is staggered so that the cable looks like little O's and little X's. It is a good example of how a simple alteration in row order can give very different results.

Panel of 12 sts.

Rows 1 and 3 (Wrong side)—K2, p8, k2.
Row 2—P2, k8, p2.
Row 4—P2, sl next 2 sts to dpn and hold in back, k2, then k2 from dpn; sl next 2 sts to dpn and hold in front, k2, then k2 from dpn; p2.
Rows 5, 6, and 7—Repeat Rows 1, 2, and 3.
Row 8—P2, sl next 2 sts to dpn and hold in front, k2, then k2 from dpn; sl next 2 sts to dpn and hold in back, k2, then k2 from dpn; p2.
Rows 9–12—Repeat Rows 5–8.
Rows 13–16—Repeat Rows 1–4.

Repeat Rows 1–16.

Hourglass Cable

The Hourglass Cable is a beautiful variation on a recurrent theme in Aran patterns. These gracefully curved lines are seen in many other combinations.

Panel of 14 sts.

Row 1 (Wrong side)—K4, p1-b, k1, p2-b, k1, p1-b, k4.
Row 2—P3, sl next st to dpn and hold in back, k1-b, then p1 from dpn (Back Cross, BC); BC again; sl next st to dpn and hold in front, p1, then k1-b from dpn (Front Cross, FC); FC again; p3.
Row 3 and all subsequent wrong-side rows—K all knit sts and p-b all purl sts.
Row 4—P2, BC, sl next st to dpn and hold in back, k1-b, then k1-b from dpn; p2, sl next st to dpn and hold in front, k1-b, then k1-b from dpn; FC, p2.
Row 6—P1, (BC) twice, FC, BC, (FC) twice, p1.
Row 8—(P1, k1-b) twice, p2, k2-b, p2, (k1-b, p1) twice.
Row 10—P1, (FC) twice, BC, FC, (BC) twice, p1.
Row 12—P2, (FC) twice, p2, (BC) twice, p2.
Row 14—P3, (FC) twice, (BC) twice, p3.
Row 16—P4, k1-b, p1, k2-b, p1, k1-b, p4.

Repeat Rows 1–16.

CENTER PANEL: *Hourglass Cable*
SIDE PANELS: *Notched Cable*

Notched Cable

This is a novelty cable suitable for use with other cable patterns. Since the design is small and rather unobtrusive, the Notched Cable is best worked in a heavy yarn on big needles so that it may show up well.

Panel of 11 sts.

Row 1 (Wrong side)—K1, p2, k2, p1, k2, p2, k1.

Row 2—P1, sl next 2 sts to dpn and hold in front, p2, then k2 from dpn; k1, sl next 2 sts to dpn and hold in back, k2, then p2 from dpn; p1.

Rows 3, 5, and 7—K3, p5, k3.

Rows 4 and 6—P3, k5, p3.

Row 8—P1, sl next 2 sts to dpn and hold in back, k2, then p2 from dpn; k1, sl next 2 sts to dpn and hold in front, p2, then k2 from dpn; p1.

Repeat Rows 1–8.

Aran Diamonds with Popcorns

Panel of 19 sts.

CENTER PANEL: *Aran Diamonds with Popcorns*
LEFT SIDE PANEL: *Flying Buttress, right*
RIGHT SIDE PANEL: *Flying Buttress, left*

NOTES: Back Cross (BC)—sl 1 p st to dpn and hold in back, k2, then p the st from dpn. Front Cross (FC)—sl 2 sts to dpn and hold in front, p1, then k2 from dpn.

Row 1 (Wrong side)—P1, k3, k in front, back, front, back, front of next st (5 sts from 1) and sl the worked st off left-hand needle (Popcorn made); k2, p2, k1, p2, k2, popcorn in next st as before, k3, p1.

Row 2—K1, p3, k5 tog-b (completing popcorn); p2, sl next 3 sts to dpn and hold in front, k2, sl the p st from dpn back to left-hand needle and p it, then k2 from dpn; p2, k5 tog-b, p3, k1.

Row 3—P1, k6, p2, k1, p2, k6, p1.

Row 4—K1, p5, BC, p1, FC, p5, k1.

Row 5—P1, k5, p2, k3, p2, k5, p1.

Row 6—K1, p4, BC, p3, FC, p4, k1.

Row 7—P1, k4, p2, k2, popcorn, k2, p2, k4, p1.

Row 8—K1, p3, BC, p2, k5 tog-b, p2, FC, p3, k1.

Row 9—P1, k3, p2, k7, p2, k3, p1.

Row 10—K1, p2, BC, p7, FC, p2, k1.

Row 11—P1, k2, p2, k2, popcorn, k3, popcorn, k2, p2, k2, p1.

Row 12—K1, p1, BC, p2, k5 tog-b, p3, k5 tog-b, p2, FC, p1, k1.

Row 13—P1, k1, p2, k11, p2, k1, p1.

Row 14—K1, p1, k2, p11, k2, p1, k1.

Row 15—P1, k1, p2, k3, popcorn, k3, popcorn, k3, p2, k1, p1.

Row 16—K1, p1, FC, p2, k5 tog-b, p3, k5 tog-b, p2, BC, p1, k1.

Row 17—P1, k2, p2, k9, p2, k2, p1.
Row 18—K1, p2, FC, p7, BC, p2, k1.
Row 19—P1, k3, p2, k3, popcorn, k3, p2, k3, p1.
Row 20—K1, p3, FC, p2, k5 tog-b, p2, BC, p3, k1.
Row 21—P1, k4, p2, k5, p2, k4, p1.
Row 22—K1, p4, FC, p3, BC, p4, k1.
Row 23 P1, k5, p2, k3, p2, k5, p1.
Row 24—K1, p5, FC, p1, BC, p5, k1.

Repeat Rows 1–24.

Panel includes 2 k sts, one on either side.

Flying Buttress

Compared to most cable patterns, the Flying Buttress is almost stark in its simplicity. It consists of a single rib of two knit stitches, traveling diagonally on a purled ground, either (1) to the right, or (2) to the left. The Right version is done with a series of back crosses, the Left with front crosses. When worked on either side of a common center, as shown, these two versions should be used, one on each side. For a Double Flying Buttress, cast on a panel of 20 stitches and work one version on the first 10, the other on the second 10—reversing the order, of course, on the opposite side of the fabric.

(1) FLYING BUTTRESS, RIGHT

(See illustration, page 26)

Panel of 10 sts.

Row 1 (Wrong side)—P2, k6, p2.
Row 2—K2, p5, sl next st to dpn and hold in back, k2, then k1 from dpn.
Row 3—P3, k5, p2.
Row 4—K2, p4, sl next st to dpn and hold in back, k2, then k1 from dpn, k1.
Row 5—P4, k4, p2.
Row 6—K2, p3, sl next st to dpn and hold in back, k2, then *p1* from dpn (Back Cross, BC), k2.
Row 7—P2, k1, p2, k3, p2.
Row 8—K2, p2, BC, p1, k2.
Row 9—(P2, k2) twice, p2.
Row 10—K2, p1, BC, p2, k2.
Row 11—P2, k3, p2, k1, p2.
Row 12—K2, BC, p3, k2.
Row 13—P2, k4, p4.
Row 14—K1, BC, p4, k2.
Row 15—P2, k5, p3.
Row 16—BC, p5, k2.

Repeat Rows 1–16.

27

(2) FLYING BUTTRESS, LEFT

(See illustration, page 26)

Panel of 10 sts.

Row 1 (Wrong side)—P2, k6, p2.
Row 2—Sl 2 sts to dpn and hold in front, k1, then k2 from dpn, p5, k2.
Row 3—P2, k5, p3.
Row 4—K1, sl next 2 sts to dpn and hold in front, k1, then k2 from dpn, p4, k2.
Row 5—P2, k4, p4.
Row 6—K2, sl next 2 sts to dpn and hold in front, *p1,* then k2 from dpn (Front Cross, FC), p3, k2.
Row 7—P2, k3, p2, k1, p2.
Row 8—K2, p1, FC, p2, k2.
Row 9—(P2, k2) twice, p2.
Row 10—K2, p2, FC, p1, k2.
Row 11—P2, k1, p2, k3, p2.
Row 12—K2, p3, FC, k2.
Row 13—P4, k4, p2.
Row 14—K2, p4, FC, k1.
Row 15—P3, k5, p2.
Row 16—K2, p5, FC.

Repeat Rows 1–16.

Figure-Eight Diamond Pattern

CENTER PANEL: *Figure-Eight Diamond Pattern*
SIDE PANELS: *Figure-Eight Cable*

Both this pattern and the Figure-Eight Cable are popular Aran designs, often used together in the same garment.

Panel of 22 sts.

Row 1 (Wrong side)—K9, p4, k9.
Row 2—P9, sl next 2 sts to dpn and hold in back, k2, then k2 from dpn; p9.
Row 3 and all subsequent wrong-side rows—Knit all knit sts and purl all purl sts.
Row 4—P8, sl next st to dpn and hold in back, k2, then p1 from dpn (Back Cross, BC); sl next 2 sts to dpn and hold in front, p1, then k2 from dpn (Front Cross, FC); p8.
Row 6—P7, BC, p2, FC, p7.
Row 8—P6, BC, p4, FC, p6.
Row 10—P5, BC, p1, k4, p1, FC, p5.
Row 12—P4, BC, p1, BC, FC, p1, FC, p4.
Row 14—P3, BC, p1, BC, p2, FC, p1, FC, p3.
Row 16—(P2, BC, p2, FC) twice, p2.
Row 18—P1, (BC, p4, FC) twice, p1.

Row 20—P1, k2, p6, sl next 2 sts to dpn and hold in back, k2, then k2 from dpn; p6, k2, p1.
Row 22—P1, (FC, p4, BC) twice, p1.
Row 24—(P2, FC, p2, BC) twice, p2.
Row 26—P3, FC, p1, FC, p2, BC, p1, BC, p3.
Row 28—P4, FC, p1, FC, BC, p1, BC, p4.
Row 30—P5, FC, p6, BC, p5.
Row 32—P6, FC, p4, BC, p6.
Row 34—P7, FC, p2, BC, p7.
Row 36—P8, FC, BC, p8.

Repeat Rows 1–36.

Figure-Eight Cable

See Figure-Eight Diamond Pattern.

Panel of 12 sts.

Row 1 (Wrong side)—K5, p2, k5.
Row 2—P4, k4, p4.
Wrong-side rows from 3 through 19—Knit all knit sts and purl all purl sts.
Row 4—P3, sl next st to dpn and hold in back, k2, then p1 from dpn (Back Cross, BC); sl next 2 sts to dpn and hold in front, p1, then k2 from dpn (Front Cross, FC); p3.
Row 6—P2, BC, p2, FC, p2.
Row 8—P2, FC, p2, BC, p2.
Row 10—P3, FC, BC, p3.
Row 12—P4, sl next 2 sts to dpn and hold in back, k2, then k2 from dpn; p4.
Rows 14, 16, 18, and 20—Repeat Rows 4, 6, 8, and 10.
Row 21—K4, p4, k4.
Rows 22, 24, and 26—P5, k2, p5.
Rows 23, 25, and 27—K5, p2, k5.
Row 28—P5, k2, p5.

Repeat Rows 1–28.

Double-Braided Cable

The construction of this cable is similar to that of Triple-Braided Diamonds, but a bit simpler, as there are only four crossing ribs instead of six.

Panel of 22 sts.

NOTES: FC (Front Cross): sl 2 sts to dpn and hold in front, p1, then k2 from dpn.

CENTER PANEL: *Double-Braided Cable*
SIDE PANELS: *Scotch Faggoting Cable*

BC (Back Cross): sl 1 st to dpn and hold in back, k2, then p1 from dpn.

FDKC (Front Double Knit Cross): sl 2 sts to dpn and hold in front, k2, then k2 from dpn.

BDKC (Back Double Knit Cross): sl 2 sts to dpn and hold in back, k2, then k2 from dpn.

Rows 1 and 3 (Wrong side)—K2, p2, k3, p2, k4, p2, k3, p2, k2.
Row 2—P2, k2, p3, k2, p4, k2, p3, k2, p2.
Row 4—P2, (FC, p2) twice, (BC, p2) twice.
Row 5 and all subsequent wrong-side rows—Knit all knit sts and purl all purl sts.
Row 6—P3, FC, p2, FC, BC, p2, BC, p3.
Row 8—P4, FC, p2, BDKC, p2, BC, p4.
Row 10—P5, (FC, BC) twice, p5.
Row 12—P6, FDKC, p2, FDKC, p6.
Row 14—P5, (BC, FC) twice, p5.
Row 16—P4, BC, p2, BDKC, p2, FC, p4.
Row 18—P3, BC, p2, BC, FC, p2, FC, p3.
Row 20—P2, (BC, p2) twice, (FC, p2) twice.
Rows 22, 24, and 26—As Row 2.

Repeat Rows 1–26.

Scotch Faggoting Cable

This novel openwork cable is rarely seen, but it is so attractive and so easy to work that the reason for its rarity can only be that it is so little known. A panel is given, but the motif is easily converted into an all-over pattern by working it on a multiple of 6 sts plus 2 (2 purl sts between cables). When repeating across the fabric, it is a good idea to begin every alternate cable with Row 9, so that the crossings will be staggered. If desired, every other cable may be worked with a back cross instead of a front cross.

Panel of 8 sts.

Row 1 (Right side)—P2, k2, yo, k2 tog, p2.
Row 2—K2, p2, yo, p2 tog, k2.
Rows 3 and 5—As Row 1.
Rows 4 and 6—As Row 2.
Row 7—P2, sl 2 to dpn and hold in front, k2, then k2 from dpn, p2.
Row 8—As Row 2.
Rows 9, 11, 13, and 15—As Row 1.
Rows 10, 12, 14, and 16—As Row 2.

Repeat Rows 1–16.

Trellis With Moss Stitch

This is another traditional Aran pattern.

Panel of 28 sts.

Row 1 (Right side)—P5, sl next 2 sts to dpn and hold in front, k2-b, then k2-b
   the sts from dpn (Front Double Knit Cross or FDKC); p10, FDKC, p5.
Row 2 and all other wrong-side rows—Knit all knit sts and purl all purl sts.
Row 3—P4, sl next st to dpn and hold in back, k2-b, then p st from dpn (Back
   Cross or BC); sl next 2 sts to dpn and hold in front, k1, then k2-b the sts from
   dpn (Front Cross or FC); p8, BC, FC, p4.
Row 5—P3, * BC, k1, p1, FC, * p6, rep from * to *, p3.
Row 7—P2, * BC, (k1, p1) twice, FC, * p4, rep from * to *, p2.
Row 9—P1, * BC, (k1, p1) 3 times, FC, * p2, rep from * to *, p1.
Row 11—* BC, (k1, p1) 4 times, FC; rep from *.
Row 13—K2-b, (k1, p1) 5 times, FDKC, (k1, p1) 5 times, k2-b.
Row 15—* Sl 2 sts to dpn and hold in front, PURL 1, then k2-b the sts from
   dpn (Front Purl Cross or FPC); (k1, p1) 4 times, BC; rep from *.
Row 17—P1, * FPC, (k1, p1) 3 times, BC, * p2, rep from * to *, p1.
Row 19—P2, * FPC, (k1, p1) twice, BC, * p4, rep from * to *, p2.
Row 21—P3, * FPC, k1, p1, BC, * p6, rep from * to *, p3.
Row 23—P4, FPC, BC, p8, FPC, BC, p4.
Row 24—See Row 2.

Repeat Rows 1–24.

A Bobble or other decoration may be worked into the purled
diamonds at the center of pattern, or these diamonds may be
formed of some other texture stitch if desired.

CENTER PANEL: *Trellis with Moss Stitch*
SIDE PANELS: *Coin Cable*

Coin Cable

This pretty little cable is made with a rather novel cabling
technique that forms small round medallions with the side
stitches crossed in front. The central portion of the "coins" is
slightly indented, instead of lifting forward as most cables do.

Panel of 9 sts.

Row 1 (Wrong side)—K2, p5, k2.
Row 2—P2, sl next 4 sts to dpn and hold in back, k1, then sl the last 3 of the sts
   from dpn back to left-hand needle; then (before knitting the sts) bring dpn with
   the last st to *front* between needles, passing to the left of the yarn; then knit the
   3 sts from left-hand needle; then knit the last st from dpn; p2.
Rows 3 and 5—Repeat Row 1.
Rows 4 and 6—P2, k5, p2.

Repeat Rows 1–6.

Fancy Bobble Cable

CENTER PANEL: *Fancy Bobble Cable*
SIDE PANELS: *Fast-Traveling Rib, or Snake Rib*

Usually bobbles are made out of one stitch, but in this pattern they are made of two stitches. This way of making bobbles is useful for any pattern that is worked on an even number of stitches, so that there are two instead of a single central stitch; when it is desirable to place a bobble in the center, it can be made from both central stitches.

Panel of 16 sts.

Row 1 (Right side)—P2, k4, p4, k4, p2.

Row 2—K2, p4, k4, p4, k2.

Row 3—P2, sl 2 sts to dpn and hold in front, k2, then k2 from dpn; p4; sl 2 sts to dpn and hold in back, k2, then k2 from dpn; p2.

Row 4—Repeat Row 2.

Row 5—P2, k4, p1, Make Bobble as follows: (k1, p1, k1) into *each* of the next 2 sts, turn and p6; turn and k1, ssk, k2 tog, k1; turn and (p2 tog) twice, turn and k2, completing Bobble; p1, k4, p2.

Rows 6, 8, and 10—Repeat Row 2.

Row 7—Repeat Row 3.

Row 9—Repeat Row 1.

Row 11—(Sl 2 sts to dpn and hold in back, k2, then p2 from dpn; sl next 2 sts to dpn and hold in front, p2, then k2 from dpn) twice.

Rows 12 and 14—P2, k4, p4, k4, p2.

Row 13—K2, p4, k4, p4, k2.

Row 15—(Sl 2 sts to dpn and hold in front, p2, then k2 from dpn; sl next 2 sts to dpn and hold in back, k2, then p2 from dpn) twice.

Row 16—Repeat Row 2.

Repeat Rows 1–16.

Fast-Traveling Rib, or Snake Rib

Most "traveling" cables move across the background one stitch at a time on every other row, the cabling action taking place on right-side rows only. This one is different. It travels "fast" because the rib is moved on every row, both right and wrong sides. Hence, the knit stitches of which the rib is composed are somewhat stretched and sleeked. This smooth, slick appearance of the ribs as they undulate across the panel does rather remind one of a snake waving its way along.

When two panels of this pattern are used on either side of a common center, as shown, one of the panels should start with Row 1 and the other with Row 13. If desired, panels can be made narrower by working over a smaller number of stitches.

Panel of 12 sts.

NOTES: Front Cross (FC): sl 2 sts to dpn and hold in front, p1, then k2 from dpn. Reverse Front Cross (RFC): sl 1 st to dpn and hold in front (i.e., at the *wrong* side, which is facing the knitter), p2, then k1 from dpn. Back Cross (BC): sl 1 st to dpn and hold in back, k2, then p1 from dpn. Reverse Back Cross (RBC): sl 2 sts to dpn and hold in back (i.e., at the *right* side, which is facing away from the knitter), k1, then p2 from dpn.

Row 1 (Wrong side)—K10, p2.
Row 2—FC, p9.
Row 3—K8, RFC, k1.
Row 4—P2, FC, p7.
Row 5—K6, RFC, k3.
Row 6—P4, FC, p5.
Row 7—K4, RFC, k5.
Row 8—P6, FC, p3.
Row 9—K2, RFC, k7.
Row 10—P8, FC, p1.
Row 11—RFC, k9.
Row 12—P10, k2.

Row 13—P2, k10.
Row 14—P9, BC.
Row 15—K1, RBC, k8.
Row 16—P7, BC, p2.
Row 17—K3, RBC, k6.
Row 18—P5, BC, p4.
Row 19—K5, RBC, k4.
Row 20—P3, BC, p6.
Row 21—K7, RBC, k2.
Row 22—P1, BC, p8.
Row 23—K9, RBC.
Row 24—K2, p10.

Repeat Rows 1–24.

Off-Center Trellis

This novel and interesting pattern incorporates moss stitch diamonds in a braided trellis pattern. Excellent for sleeve panels or elsewhere in fancy sweaters.

Panel of 25 sts.

NOTES: Front Purl Cross or FPC sl 2 k sts to dpn, hold in front, p1, then k2 from dpn.

Back Purl Cross or BPC—sl 1 p st to dpn, hold in back, k2, then p1 from dpn.

Front Knit Cross or FKC—sl 2 k sts to dpn, hold in front, k1, then k2 from dpn.

Front Double Knit Cross or FDKC—sl 2 k sts to dpn, hold in front, k2, then k2 from dpn.

Back Double Knit Cross or BDKC—sl 2 k sts to dpn, hold in back, k2, then k2 from dpn.

CENTER PANEL: *Off-Center Trellis*
SIDE PANELS: *Open Cable*

33

Row 1 (Wrong side)—P2, k6, p4, (k1, p1) 3 times, p4, k3.
Row 2—P2, BPC, FPC, (k1, p1) twice, BPC, FKC, p4, BPC.
Row 3 and all other wrong-side rows—Knit all knit sts and purl all purl sts.
Row 4—P1, BPC, p2, FPC, k1, p1, BPC, k1, p1, FKC, p2, BPC, p1.
Row 6—BPC, p4, FPC, BPC, (k1, p1) twice, FKC, BPC, p2.
Row 8—K2, P6, BDKC, (k1, p1) 3 times, BDKC, p3.
Row 10—FPC, p4, BPC, FKC, (k1, p1) twice, BPC, FPC, p2.
Row 12—P1, FPC, p2, BPC, k1, p1, FKC, k1, p1, BPC, p2, FPC, p1.
Row 14—P2, FPC, BPC, (k1, p1) twice, FKC, BPC, p4, FPC.
Row 16—P3, FDKC, (k1, p1) 3 times, FDKC, p6, k2.

Repeat Rows 1–16.

Open Cable   *(See illustration, page 33)*

This is a traditional and very handsome form of cable, sometimes made with a Bobble worked in the central stitch on Row 8.

Panel of 11 sts.

Row 1 (Wrong side)—K3, p2, k1, p2, k3.
Row 2—P3, sl next 3 to dpn and hold in back, k2, sl the p st back to left-hand
    needle and p it, k2 from dpn, p3.
Row 3—As Row 1.
Row 4—P2, sl next p st to dpn and hold in back, k2, p the st from dpn (*Back
    Cross*); p1, sl next 2 to dpn and hold in front, p1, k2 from dpn (*Front Cross*); p2.
Row 5—K2, p2, k3, p2, k2.
Row 6—P1, *BC,* p3, *FC,* p1.
Row 7—K1, p2, k5, p2, k1.
Row 8—P1, k2, p5, k2, p1.
Row 9—As Row 7.
Row 10—P1, *FC,* p3, *BC,* p1.
Row 11—K2, p2, k3, p2, k2.
Row 12—P2, *FC,* p1, *BC,* p2.

Repeat Rows 1–12.

Aran Diamonds with Moss Stitch

More than any other pattern, this one typifies Aran knitting. It is pure, classic Aran: a fully developed design, symmetrical, clean, and refined by generations down to a deceptive simplicity. Sometimes it is worked on a panel of 15 stitches, with the borders of the diamonds made of two knit stitches instead of one.

Panel of 13 sts.

Row 1 (Wrong side)—K5, p1, k1, p1, k5.

Row 2—P5, sl next 2 sts to dpn and hold in front, k1-b, then sl the purl st from dpn to left-hand needle and purl it, then k1-b from dpn; p5.

Row 3—Repeat Row 1.

Row 4—P4, sl next st to dpn and hold in back, k1-b, then p1 from dpn (Back Cross, BC); k1; sl next st to dpn and hold in front, p1, then k1-b from dpn (Front Cross, FC); p4.

Row 5 and all subsequent wrong-side rows—Knit all knit sts and purl all purl sts.

Row 6—P3, BC, k1, p1, k1, FC, p3.

Row 8—P2, BC, (k1, p1) twice, k1, FC, p2.

Row 10—P1, BC, (k1, p1) 3 times, k1, FC, p1.

Row 12—BC, (k1, p1) 4 times, k1, FC.

Row 14—FC, (p1, k1) 4 times, p1, BC.

Row 16—P1, FC, (p1, k1) 3 times, p1, BC, p1.

Row 18—P2, FC, (p1, k1) twice, p1, BC, p2.

Row 20—P3, FC, p1, k1, p1, BC, p3.

Row 22—P4, FC, p1, BC, p4.

Repeat Rows 1–22.

CENTER PANEL: *Aran Diamonds with Moss Stitch*
LEFT SIDE PANEL: *Uneven Cable, front cross*
RIGHT SIDE PANEL: *Uneven Cable, back cross*

Uneven Cable

This is an archaic form of Simple Cable, an "ancestral cable" as it were. Long ago all cables were worked on uneven stitches, the larger number of stitches being crossed in front and a smaller number behind. Today, most cables cross half-and-half, which gives a tighter twist to the cable. However, the Uneven Cable is interesting and a little different, for the very reason that it is so seldom used in modern times.

Panel of 10 sts.

Rows 1, 3, and 5 (Wrong side)—K2, p6, k2.

Row 2—P2, k6, p2.

Row 4—For a Back Cross cable (twist to the right) work Row 4 as follows: p2, sl next 2 sts to dpn and hold in back, k4, then k2 from dpn, p2. For a Front Cross cable (twist to the left) work Row 4 as follows: p2, sl next 4 sts to dpn and hold in front, k2, then k4 from dpn, p2.

Row 6—Repeat Row 2.

Repeat Rows 1–6.

Double Zigzag

CENTER PANEL: *Double Zigzag*
LEFT SIDE PANEL: *Crossed Cable, front*
RIGHT SIDE PANEL: *Crossed Cable, back*

This is a basic pattern; the knit zigzag ribs on a background of purl occur in dozens of different shapes and sizes. Sometimes the ribs are made of a single stitch instead of two stitches. Sometimes there are only two zigzagging ribs instead of four; sometimes there are six (three on each side) or eight (four on each side) or more. Sometimes there is a central rib worked vertically straight. Sometimes there are more pattern rows, hence longer zigzags. (See also Fast-Traveling Rib.)

Panel of 20 sts.

NOTES: Back Cross (BC): sl 1 st to dpn and hold in back, k2, then p1 from dpn. Front Cross (FC): sl 2 sts to dpn and hold in front, p1, then k2 from dpn.

Row 1 (Wrong side)—K3, p2, k3, p4, k3, p2, k3.
Row 2—(P2, BC) twice, (FC, p2) twice.
Row 3 and all subsequent wrong-side rows—Knit all knit sts and purl all purl sts.
Row 4—P1, (BC, p2) twice, FC, p2, FC, p1.
Row 6—(BC, p2) twice, (p2, FC) twice.
Row 8—(FC, p2) twice, (p2, BC) twice.
Row 10—P1, (FC, p2) twice, BC, p2, BC, p1.
Row 12—(P2, FC) twice, (BC, p2) twice.

Repeat Rows 1–12.

Crossed Cable

This pretty branch-like cable can be worked with a back cross, as given, or with a front cross by substituting "hold in front" for "hold in back" in Row 1. For two cables symmetrically balanced, cross one in back, the other in front.

Panel of 12 sts.

Row 1 (Right side)—P4, sl 2 to dpn and hold in back, k2, then k2 from dpn, p4.
Row 2—K4, p4, k4.
Row 3—P3, sl 1 to dpn and hold in back, k2, then k1 from dpn (Back Cross or BC); sl next 2 to dpn and hold in front, k1, then k2 from dpn (Front Cross or FC), p3.
Row 4—K3, p6, k3.
Row 5—P2, BC, k2, FC, p2.
Row 6—K2, p8, k2.
Row 7—P1, BC, k4, FC, p1.
Row 8—K1, p10, k1.

Repeat Rows 1–8.

Box Cable

This is an unusual form of Double Cable, incorporating ridges of Garter Stitch to widen the pattern. The panel is alternately extended and tightened from side to side, so that the border stitches will take on a slight wave.

CENTER PANEL: *Box Cable*
SIDE PANELS: *Lovers' Knot*

Panel of 16 sts.

Row 1 (Right side)—P2, k2, p2, k4, p2, k2, p2.
Row 2—K2, p2, k2, p4, k2, p2, k2.
Rows 3 and 5—Repeat Row 1.
Rows 4 and 6—Repeat Row 2.
Row 7—P2, sl next 4 sts to dpn and hold in back, k2, then p2 and k2 from dpn; sl next 2 sts to dpn and hold in front, k2, p2, then k2 from dpn; p2.
Rows 8 and 10—Repeat Row 2.
Rows 9 and 11—Repeat Row 1.
Rows 12, 13, 14, 15, and 16—Knit.

Repeat Rows 1–16.

Lovers' Knot

This is a delightful old French pattern that can be used not only in a cable panel but also as a spot-pattern to decorate a purl fabric. It is related to a Zigzag Rib but has a few unique touches.

Panel of 9 sts.

Row 1 (Wrong side)—(P1, k3) twice, p1.
Row 2—Sl 1 st to dpn and hold in front, p1, then k1 from dpn (Front Cross, FC); p2, k1, p2, sl 1 st to dpn and hold in back, k1, then p1 from dpn (Back Cross, BC).
Rows 3, 5, 7, 9, 11, 13, and 15—Knit all knit sts and purl all purl sts.
Row 4—P1, FC, p1, k1, p1, BC, p1.
Row 6—P2, FC, k1, BC, p2.
Row 8—P2, BC, k1, FC, p2.
Row 10—P1, BC, p1, k1, p1, FC, p1.
Row 12—Repeat Row 4.
Row 14—Repeat Row 6.
Row 16—P3, left running thread between the st just worked and the next st, and purl into the back of this thread (Make One purlwise); sl 1—k2 tog—psso, Make One purlwise, p3.
Rows 17 and 19—Knit.
Rows 18 and 20—Purl.

Repeat Rows 1–20.

Bobble Fans

Panel of 15 sts.

Row 1 (Right side)—Purl.

Row 2—Knit.

Row 3—P7, Make Bobble (MB) as follows: (k1, yo, k1, yo, k1) in next st, turn and p5, turn and k5, turn and p2 tog, p1, p2 tog; turn and sl 1—k2 tog—psso, completing Bobble; p7.

Row 4—K7, p1-b, k7.

Row 5—P4, MB, p2, k1-b, p2, MB, p4.

Row 6—K4, p1-b, k2, p1, k2, p1-b, k4.

Row 7—P2, MB, p1, sl next st to dpn and hold in front, p1, then k1 from dpn (Front Cross, FC); p1, k1-b, p1, sl next st to dpn and hold in back, k1, then p1 from dpn (Back Cross, BC); p1, MB, p2.

Row 8—K2, p1-b, k2, (p1, k1) 3 times, k1, p1-b, k2.

Row 9—P2, FC, p1, FC, k1-b, BC, p1, BC, p2.

Row 10—K3, BC, k1, p3, k1, FC, k3.

Row 11—P4, FC, Make One (M1) purlwise by lifting running thread and purling into the *back* of this thread; sl 1—k2 tog—psso, M1 purlwise, BC, p4.

Row 12—K5, BC, p1, FC, k5.

Row 13—P5, purl into front and back of next st, sl 1—k2 tog—psso, purl into front and back of next st, p5.

Row 14—K7, p1, k7.

Rows 15 and 16—Repeat Rows 1 and 2.

Repeat Rows 1–16.

CENTER PANEL: *Bobble Fans*
SIDE PANELS: *Little Twist Cable*

Little Twist Cable

Panel of 10 sts.

Rows 1 and 3 (Wrong side)—K2, p6, k2.

Row 2—P2, sl next st to dpn and hold in front, k2, then k1 from dpn; sl next 2 sts to dpn and hold in back, k1, then k2 from dpn; p2.

Row 4—P2, k2, k2 tog but do not slip from needle; insert right-hand needle between the sts just knitted tog and knit the 1st st again; then sl both sts from needle together; k2, p2.

Repeat Rows 1–4.

Birdcage Cable

Panel of 22 sts.

NOTES: Front Cross (FC)—sl 1 st to dpn and hold in front, p1, then k1 from dpn. Front Knit Cross (FKC)—same as FC, but *knit* both sts. Back Cross (BC)—sl 1 st to dpn and hold in back, k1, then p1 from dpn. Back Knit Cross (BKC)—same as BC, but *knit* both sts.

Row 1 (Wrong side)—K10, p2, k10.
Row 2—P9, BKC, FKC, p9.
Row 3—K8, FC, p2, BC, k8.
Row 4—P7, BC, BKC, FKC, FC, p7.
Row 5—K6, FC, k1, p4, k1, BC, k6.
Row 6—P5, BC, p1, BC, k2, FC, p1, FC, p5.
Row 7—K4, FC, k2, p1, k1, p2, k1, p1, k2, BC, k4.
Row 8—P3, BC, p2, BC, p1, k2, p1, FC, p2, FC, p3.
Rows 9, 11, 13, 14, 15, 17, and 19—Knit all knit sts and purl all purl sts.
Row 10—(P2, BC) twice, p2, k2, p2, (FC, p2) twice.
Row 12—P1, BC, (p2, BC) twice, (FC, p2) twice, FC, p1.
Row 16—P1, FC, (p2, FC) twice, (BC, p2) twice, BC, p1.
Row 18—(P2, FC) twice, p2, k2, p2, (BC, p2) twice.
Row 20—P3, FC, p2, FC, p1, k2, p1, BC, p2, BC, p3.
Row 21—K4, BC, k2, p1, k1, p2, k1, p1, k2, FC, k4.
Row 22—P5, FC, p1, FC, k2, BC, p1, BC, p5.
Row 23—K6, BC, k1, p4, k1, FC, k6.
Row 24—P7, (FC) twice, (BC) twice, p7.
Row 25—K8, BC, p2, FC, k8.
Row 26—P9, FC, BC, p9.
Row 27—K10, p2, k10.
Row 28—P10, k2, p10.

Repeat Rows 1–28.

CENTER PANEL: *Birdcage Cable*
SIDE PANELS: *Two-Texture Rib*

Two-Texture Rib

This is a traveling rib pattern that alternates half-diamonds of purl and moss stitch. If there are two panels in symmetrical opposition, the pattern should be reversed in one of them.

Panel of 7 sts.

Row 1 (Wrong side)—K5, p2.
Row 2—Sl 2 sts to dpn and hold in front, p1, then k2 from dpn (Front Cross, FC); p4.
Row 3 and all other wrong-side rows—Knit all knit sts and purl all purl sts.
Row 4—K1, FC, p3.
Row 6—P1, k1, FC, p2.

Row 8—K1, p1, k1, FC, p1.
Row 10—(P1, k1) twice, FC.
Row 12—(K1, p1) twice, sl next st to dpn and hold in back, k2, then p1 from dpn (Back Cross, BC).
Row 14—P1, k1, p1, BC, p1.
Row 16—K1, p1, BC, p2.
Row 18—P1, BC, p3.
Row 20—BC, p4.

Repeat Rows 1–20.

Banana Tree

Panel of 18 sts.

NOTES: Front Cross (FC)—sl 1 st to dpn and hold in front, p1, then k1 from dpn. Front Knit Cross (FKC)—same as FC, but *knit* both sts. Front Purl Cross (FPC)—same as FC, but *purl* both sts.

Back Cross (BC)—sl 1 st to dpn and hold in back, k1, then p1 from dpn. Back Knit Cross (BKC)—same as BC, but *knit* both sts. Back Purl Cross (BPC)—same as BC, but *purl* both sts.

Row 1 (Wrong side)—K2, p3, k3, p4, BPC, k4.
Row 2—P3, BKC, k1, BC, k2, p3, FC, k1, p2.
Row 3—K2, p2, k4, p2, k1, p3, BPC, k2.
Row 4—P2, k3, BC, p1, k1, FKC, p3, FC, p2.
Row 5—K6, FPC, p2, k2, p4, k2.
Row 6—P2, k2, BC, p2, k1, (FKC) twice, p5.
Row 7—K4, FPC, p4, k3, p3, k2.
Row 8—P2, k1, BC, p3, k2, FC, k1, FKC, p3.
Row 9—K2, FPC, p3, k1, p2, k4, p2, k2.
Row 10—P2, BC, p3, BKC, k1, p1, FC, k3, p2.
Row 11—K2, p4, k2, p2, BPC, k6.
Row 12—P5, (BKC) twice, k1, p2, FC, k2, p2.

Repeat Rows 1–12.

LEFT: *Banana Tree*
RIGHT: *Nosegay Pattern*

Nosegay Pattern

Panel of 16 sts.

NOTES: Front Cross (FC)—sl 1 st to dpn and hold in front, p1, then k1 from dpn. Front Knit Cross (FKC)—same as FC, but *knit* both sts. Back Cross (BC)—sl 1 st to dpn and hold in back, k1, then p1 from dpn. Back Knit Cross (BKC)—same as BC, but *knit* both sts.

Row 1 (Wrong side)—K7, p2, k7.
Row 2—P6, BKC, FKC, p6.
Row 3—K5, FC, p2, BC, k5.
Row 4—P4, BC, BKC, FKC, FC, p4.
Row 5—K3, FC, k1, p4, k1, BC, k3.
Row 6—P2, BC, p1, BC, k2, FC, p1, FC, p2.
Row 7—(K2, p1) twice, k1, p2, k1, (p1, k2) twice.
Row 8—P2, Make Bobble (MB) as follows: (k1, p1) twice into next st, turn and p4, turn and k4, turn and (p2 tog) twice, turn and k2 tog, completing Bobble; p1, BC, p1, k2, p1, FC, p1, MB, p2.
Row 9—K4, p1, k2, p2, k2, p1, k4.
Row 10—P4, MB, p2, k2, p2, MB, p4.

Repeat Rows 1–10.

Rope and Diamond

Here is a classic Aran diamond pattern enlivened by a simple 4-stitch cable up the middle. It is pleasing with vertical borders also made of 4-stitch cables on each side.

Panel of 18 sts.

NOTES: Front Cross (FC): sl 2 sts to dpn and hold in front, p1, then k2 from dpn.

Back Cross (BC): sl 1 st to dpn and hold in back, k2, then p1 from dpn.

Back Knit Cross (BKC): sl 2 sts to dpn and hold in back, k2, then k2 from dpn.

Row 1 (Wrong side)—K7, p4, k7.
Row 2—P6, BC *knitting all 3 sts,* FC *knitting all 3 sts,* p6.
Row 3 and all subsequent wrong-side rows—Knit all knit sts and purl all purl sts.
Row 4—P5, BC *knitting all 3 sts,* k2, FC *knitting all 3 sts,* p5.
Row 6—P4, BC, BKC, FC, p4.
Row 8—P3, BC, p1, k4, p1, FC, p3.
Row 10—P2, BC, p2, BKC, p2, FC, p2.
Row 12—P1, BC, p3, k4, p3, FC, p1.
Row 14—P1, k2, p4, BKC, p4, k2, p1.
Row 16—P1, FC, p3, k4, p3, BC, p1.
Row 18—P2, FC, p2, BKC, p2, BC, p2.
Row 20—P3, FC, p1, k4, p1, BC, p3.
Row 22—P4, FC, BKC, BC, p4.
Row 24—P5, FC, k2, BC, p5.
Row 26—P6, FC, BC, p6.
Row 28—P7, sl next 2 sts to dpn and hold in front, k2, then k2 from dpn, p7.

Repeat Rows 1–28.

LEFT: *Rope and Diamond*
CENTER: *Ripple and Rock*
RIGHT: *Raveled Braid*

Ripple and Rock

In this simple and pretty bobble cable, the bobble is unexpectedly placed in the *smaller* of the two diamond shapes, which gives a rather novel effect. The pattern is good in central sleeve panels. With a background worked in garter stitch instead of plain purl as shown, it makes a delightful buttonhole band for a cardigan—the buttonholes being placed in the middle of the larger diamonds.

Panel of 17 sts.

NOTES: Front Cross (FC) and Back Cross (BC): Same as for Rope and Diamond.

41

Row 1 (Wrong side)—K6, p2, k1, p2, k6.

Row 2—P5, BC, p1, FC, p5.

Row 3 and all subsequent wrong-side rows except Row 7—Knit all knit sts and purl all purl sts.

Row 4—P4, BC, p3, FC, p4.

Row 6—P4, k2, p2, Make Bobble in next st as follows: (k1, yo, k1, yo, k1) in same st, turn and p5, turn and k5, turn and p2 tog, p1, p2 tog, turn and sl 1—k2 tog—psso, completing Bobble; p2, k2, p4.

Row 7—K4, p2, k2, p1-b, k2, p2, k4.

Row 8—P4, FC, p3, BC, p4.

Row 10—P5, FC, p1, BC, p5.

Rows 12 and 14—Repeat Rows 2 and 4.

Row 16—P3, BC, p5, FC, p3.

Row 18—P2, BC, p7, FC, p2.

Row 20—P2, FC, p7, BC, p2.

Row 22—P3, FC, p5, BC, p3.

Rows 24 and 26—Repeat Rows 8 and 10.

Repeat Rows 1–26.

Raveled Braid

A plain plait cable is here "raveled out" at intervals to show its three component ribs. This cable combines well with wider and fancier ones.

Panel of 16 sts.

NOTES: Front Cross (FC), Back Cross (BC) and Back Knit Cross (BKC): Same as for Rope and Diamond.

Front Knit Cross (FKC): sl 2 sts to dpn and hold in front, k2, then k2 from dpn.

Row 1 (Wrong side) —K5, p6, k5.

Rows 2, 6, and 10—P5, k2, BKC, p5.

Row 3 and all subsequent wrong-side rows—Knit all knit sts and purl all purl sts.

Rows 4, 8, and 12—P5, FKC, k2, p5.

Row 14—P4, BC, k2, FC, p4.

Row 16—P3, BC, p1, k2, p1, FC, p3.

Row 18—P2, BC, p2, k2, p2, FC, p2.

Row 20—P2, FC, p2, k2, p2, BC, p2.

Row 22—P3, FC, p1, k2, p1, BC, p3.

Row 24—P4, FC, k2, BC, p4.

Repeat Rows 1–24.

Two Fancy Open Cables:
Open Cable with Waved Rib, and Four-Rib Braid

I. OPEN CABLE WITH WAVED RIB

NOTES: Back Cross (BC): sl 1 st to dpn and hold in back, k2, then p1 from dpn.

Front Cross (FC): sl 2 sts to dpn and hold in front, p1, then k2 from dpn.

Single Back Cross (SBC): sl 1 st to dpn and hold in back, k1, then p1 from dpn.

Single Front Cross (SFC): sl 1 st to dpn and hold in front, p1, then k1 from dpn.

Fancy Open Cables
LEFT: *Open Cable with Waved Rib*
RIGHT: *Four-Rib Braid*

Panel of 15 sts.

Row 1 (Wrong side)—K2, p1, k2, p2, k1, p2, k2, p1, k2.
Row 2—P2, k1, p2, sl next 3 sts to dpn and hold in back, k2, then sl the purl st from dpn back to left-hand needle and purl it, then k2 from dpn; p2, k1, p2.
Row 3—Repeat Row 1.
Row 4—P2, SFC, BC, p1, FC, SBC, p2.
Rows 5 and 7—(K3, p3) twice, k3.
Row 6—P3, work BC but knit all 3 sts, p3, work FC but knit all 3 sts, p3.
Row 8—P2, BC, SFC, p1, SBC, FC, p2.
Rows 9 and 11—K2, p2, k2, p1, k1, p1, k2, p2, k2.
Row 10—P2, k2, p2, k1, p1, k1, p2, k2, p2.
Row 12—P2, FC, SBC, p1, SFC, BC, p2.
Rows 13 and 15 Repeat Rows 5 and 7.
Row 14—P3, work FC but knit all 3 sts, p3, work BC but knit all 3 sts, p3.
Row 16—P2, SBC, FC, p1, BC, SFC, p2.

Repeat Rows 1–16.

II. FOUR-RIB BRAID

NOTES: BC and FC—same as given for Open Cable with Waved Rib.

Panel of 17 sts.

Row 1 (Wrong side)—(K2, p2) twice, k1, (p2, k2) twice.
Row 2—P2, k2, p2, sl next 3 sts to dpn and hold in back, k2, sl the purl st from dpn back to left-hand needle and purl it, then k2 from dpn; p2, k2, p2.
Row 3—Repeat Row 1.
Row 4—P2, FC, BC, p1, FC, BC, p2.
Row 5—(K3, p4) twice, k3.
Row 6 P3, sl next 2 sts to dpn and hold in back, k2, then k2 from dpn; p3, sl next 2 sts to dpn and hold in front, k2, then k2 from dpn; p3.
Row 7—Repeat Row 5.

Row 8—P2, BC, FC, p1, BC, FC, p2.
Row 9—Repeat Row 1.
Row 10—P2, k2, p2, sl the next 3 sts to dpn and hold in *front*, k2, then sl the purl st from dpn back to left-hand needle and purl it, then k2 from dpn; p2, k2, p2.
Rows 11 through 16—Repeat Rows 3 through 8.

Repeat Rows 1–16.

Framed Cable

LEFT: *Framed Cable*
CENTER: *Ensign's Braid*
RIGHT: *Sausage Cable*

Try this graceful pattern instead of a simple cable in a tennis sweater or similar "classic" garment. The Framed Cable is remarkably elegant, too, as a border for a cardigan or a single sleeve panel. This is one of those why-didn't-*I*-think-of-that patterns, with exceedingly simple elements that happen to combine very successfully. (No, your author *didn't* think of it. It is an English pattern.)

Panel of 18 sts.

NOTES: Front Cross (FC): sl 3 sts to dpn and hold in front, k3, then k3 from dpn.

Single Front Cross (SFC): sl 1 st to dpn and hold in front, p1, then k1-b from dpn.

Single Back Cross (SBC): sl 1 st to dpn and hold in back, k1-b, then p1 from dpn.

Row 1 (Wrong side)—K5, p8, k5.
Row 2—P4, SBC, k6, SFC, p4.
Row 3 and all subsequent wrong-side rows—Knit all knit sts and purl all purl sts.
Row 4—P3, SBC, p1, k6, p1, SFC, p3.
Row 6—P2, SBC, p2, FC, p2, SFC, p2.
Row 8—P1, SBC, p3, k6, p3, SFC, p1.
Row 10—P1, SFC, p3, k6, p3, SBC, p1.
Row 12—P2, SFC, p2, FC, p2, SBC, p2.
Row 14—P3, SFC, p1, k6, p1, SBC, p3.
Row 16—P4, SFC, k6, SBC, p4.

Repeat Rows 1–16.

Ensign's Braid

This is an enlarged Four-Rib Braid with a different arrangement of the cabled crossings. There are two superimposed diamonds, the upper one crossing to the left and the lower to the right. The effect is intricate, although the working of the pattern is not.

Panel of 24 sts.

NOTES: Front Cross (FC): sl 3 sts to dpn and hold in front, k3, then k3 from dpn.

Back Cross (BC): sl 3 sts to dpn and hold in back, k3, then k3 from dpn.

Single Front Cross (SFC): sl 3 sts to dpn and hold in front, p1, then k3 from dpn.

Single Back Cross (SBC): sl 1 st to dpn and hold in back, k3, then p1 from dpn.

Row 1 (Wrong side)—K2, p3, k4, p6, k4, p3, k2.
Row 2—P2, k3, p4, BC, p4, k3, p2.
Row 3 and all subsequent wrong-side rows—Knit all knit sts and purl all purl sts.
Row 4—P2, (SFC, p2, SBC) twice, p2.
Row 6—P3, SFC, SBC, p2, SFC, SBC, p3.
Row 8—P4, FC, p4, BC, p4.
Row 10—P3, SBC, SFC, p2, SBC, SFC, p3.
Row 12—P2, (SBC, p2, SFC) twice, p2.
Row 14—P2, k3, p4, FC, p4, k3, p2.
Rows 16 and 18—Repeat Rows 4 and 6.
Row 20—P4, BC, p4, FC, p4.
Rows 22 and 24—Repeat Rows 10 and 12.

Repeat Rows 1–24.

Sausage Cable

This cable is made in long ovals with three little crossings in the center of each. The novel touch is seen in the method of decreasing and increasing between the "links".

Panel of 12 sts.

Rows 1, 3, 5, 7, 9, and 11 (Wrong side)—K2, p8, k2.
Row 2—P2, k2, sl next 2 sts to dpn and hold in front, k2, then k2 from dpn; k2, p2.
Rows 4 and 8—P2, k8, p2.
Rows 6 and 10—Repeat Row 2.
Row 12—P2, k2, k2 tog, ssk, k2, p2.
Row 13—K2, p6, k2.
Row 14—P2, k1, ssk, k2 tog, k1, p2.
Rows 15 and 17—K2, p4, k2.
Row 16—P2, sl next 2 sts to dpn and hold in back, k2, then k2 from dpn; p2.
Row 18—P2, k1, M1, k2, M1, k1, p2.
Row 19—Repeat Row 13.
Row 20—P2, (k2, M1) twice, k2, p2.

Repeat Rows 1–20.

LEFT: *Lobster Claw*
CENTER: *Giant Embossed Plait*
RIGHT: *Elliptical Cable*

Lobster Claw

Panel of 12 sts.

Row 1 (Wrong side)—Knit.
Row 2—P2, k1, p6, k1, p2.
Rows 3, 5, and 7—K2, p2, k4, p2, k2.
Rows 4 and 6—P2, k2, p4, k2, p2.
Row 8—P2, sl next 2 sts to dpn and hold in front, p2, yo, then k2 tog-b from dpn; sl next 2 sts to dpn and hold in back, k2 tog, yo, then p2 from dpn; p2.

Repeat Rows 1–8.

Giant Embossed Plait

Contributed by Grace E. Smith, LaVerne, California

This is a huge and heavy plait pattern made by a highly unusual method. Each of the plaited ribs is a series of short rows, and each one stands up a full quarter-inch, or more, from the background. If several of these giant plaits are being worked at once, then a separate cable needle will be required for each, because the stitches are left on the cable needle throughout an entire right-side row, and are not picked up again until the return row. (If you want to use a number of Giant Embossed Plaits but do not have a sufficient number of cable needles, round toothpicks will do nicely instead.)

Panel of 16 sts.

Preparation Row (Wrong side)—Purl.
Row 1—K10, (turn, p4, turn, k4) 3 times; then sl these 4 sts to dpn and leave at front of work. Pass yarn to back between needles, sl 4 sts from right-hand needle to left-hand needle, k10.
Row 2—P10, p4 from dpn, p2.
Row 3—K10, (turn, p4, turn, k4) 3 times; then sl these 4 sts to dpn and leave at front of work. Pass yarn to back between needles, sl 4 sts from left-hand needle to right-hand needle, k2.
Row 4—P2, p4 from dpn, p10.

Repeat Rows 1–4.

Elliptical Cable

Panel of 12 sts.

Row 1 (Wrong side) and all other wrong-side rows—K2, p2-b, p4, p2-b, k2.
Row 2—P2, k2-b, k4, k2-b, p2.

Row 4—P2, k2-b, sl next 2 sts to dpn and hold in back, k2, then k2 from dpn; k2-b, p2.

Rows 6 and 8—Repeat Row 2.

Row 10—P2, sl next 4 sts to dpn and hold in back, k2, then knit 1st 2 sts from dpn; bring dpn with remaining 2 sts through to front of work, k2, then k2 from dpn; p2.

Repeat Rows 1–10.

Nautical Twisted-Rope Cable

Contributed by Pauline Balbes, Hollywood, California

Big, bold, and bulky! This "giant" is wonderful for Aran-knit coats, jackets, sweaters and afghans. The panel includes the little four-stitch simple cables on each side, plus four more edge stitches.

Panel of 49 sts.

NOTES: Front Cross (FC): sl 2 sts to dpn and hold in front, k2, then k2 from dpn.

Back Cross (BC): sl 2 sts to dpn and hold in back, k2, then k2 from dpn.

Make One (M1): pick up running thread before next st and purl into the *back* of this thread.

Row 1 (Right side)—(P2, k4) 4 times, p1, (k4, p2) 4 times.

Rows 2, 4, 6, and 8—(K2, p4) 4 times, k1, (p4, k2) 4 times.

Row 3—(P2, FC, p2, k4) twice, p1, (k4, p2, BC, p2) twice.

Row 5—Repeat Row 1.

CENTER PANEL: *Nautical Twisted-Rope Cable*
SIDE PANELS: *Dry Bones Cable*

Row 7—P2, FC, p2, k4, p2, FC, p2, sl next 5 sts to dpn and hold in front, k4, then sl the purl st from dpn back to left-hand needle and purl it; then k4 from dpn; p2, BC, p2, k4, p2, BC, p2.

Row 9—P2, k4, p2, * M1, (k4, p2) twice, k4, M1 *, p1, repeat from * to *, p2, k4, p2.

Row 10—K2, p4, * k3, p4, (k2, p4) twice, rep from *, k3, p4, k2.

Row 11—P2, FC, p3, M1, k4, p2 tog, FC, p2 tog, k4, M1, p3, M1, k4, p2 tog, BC, p2 tog, k4, M1, p3, BC, p2.

Row 12—K2, p4, k4, * (p4, k1) twice, p4 *, k5, rep from * to *, k4, p4, k2.

Row 13—P2, k4, p4, * M1, k3, ssk, k4, k2 tog, k3, M1 *, p5, rep from * to *, p4, k4, p2.

Row 14—K2, p4, k5, p12, k7, p12, k5, p4, k2.

Row 15—P2, FC, p5, M1, k4, FC, k4, M1, p7, M1, k4, BC, k4, M1, p5, BC, p2.

Row 16—K2, p4, k6, p12, k9, p12, k6, p4, k2.

Row 17—P2, k4, p6, sl next 8 sts to dpn and hold in back, k4, then sl the 2nd 4 sts from dpn back to left-hand needle and knit them; then k4 from dpn; p9, sl next 8 sts to dpn and hold in front, k4, then sl the 2nd 4 sts from dpn back to left-hand needle and knit them; then k4 from dpn; p6, k4, p2.

Rows 18, 20, 22, and 24—Repeat Rows 16, 14, 12, and 10.

Row 19—P2, FC, p4, p2 tog, k4, FC, k4, p2 tog, p5, p2 tog, k4, BC, k4, p2 tog, p4, BC, p2.

Row 21—P2, k4, p3, * p2 tog, (k4, M1) twice, k4, p2 tog, p3, rep from *, k4, p2.

Row 23—P2, FC, p2, p2 tog, k4, M1, p1, FC, p1, M1, k4, p2 tog, p1, p2 tog, k4, M1, p1, BC, p1, M1, k4, p2 tog, p2, BC, p2.

Row 25—P2, k4, p1, p2 tog, * (k4, p2) twice, k4 *, p3 tog, rep from * to *, p2 tog, p1, k4, p2.

Row 26—Repeat Row 2.

Row 27—Repeat Row 7.

Row 28—Repeat Row 2.

Repeat Rows 1–28.

Dry Bones Cable

In strong contrast to the Nautical Twisted-Rope, this cable is about as skeletal and skinny as a cable can be. But its slender lines of single stitches suggest the wider motif that would result if these "bones" were fleshed out with seven knit stitches instead of the solitary one in the center.

Panel of 11 sts.

Notes: Front Cross (FC): sl 1 st to dpn and hold in front, p1, then k1-b from dpn.

Back Cross (BC): sl 1 st to dpn and hold in back, k1-b, then p1 from dpn.

Rows 1 and 3 (Right side)—P5, k1-b, p5.

Row 2—K5, p1, k5.

Row 4—K2, (p1, k2) 3 times.

Row 5—P2, (k1-b, p2) 3 times.

Row 6—K2, p1, k5, p1, k2.

Row 7—P2, FC, p3, BC, p2.

Rows 8 and 10—K3, (p1, k3) twice.

Row 9—P3, sl next 4 sts to dpn and hold in front, drop next st off left-hand needle; sl the 3 purl sts from dpn back to left-hand needle, then with point of dpn pick up dropped st and place it on left-hand needle after the 3 purl sts; then k1, p3 from left-hand needle; then k1-b from dpn; p3.

Row 11—P2, BC, p3, FC, p2.

Rows 12, 13, 14, 15, and 16—Repeat Rows 6, 5, 4, 3, and 2.

Repeat Rows 1–16.

Hartshorn Cable

Panel of 28 sts.

NOTES: Front Cross (FC)—sl 2 sts to dpn and hold in front, p2, then k2 from dpn.

Front Knit Cross (FKC)—same as FC, but *knit* all 4 sts.

Back Cross (BC)—sl 2 sts to dpn and hold in back, k2, then p2 from dpn.

Back Knit Cross (BKC)—same as BC, but *knit* all 4 sts.

Single Front Cross (SFC)—sl 2 sts to dpn and hold in front, p1, then k2 from dpn.

Single Back Cross (SBC)—sl 1 st to dpn and hold in back, k2, then p1 from dpn.

Rows 1 and 3 (Wrong side)—K9, p10, k9.
Row 2—P9, BKC, k2, FKC, p9.
Row 4—P7, BC, k2, BKC, FC, p7.
Row 5 and all other wrong-side rows—Knit all knit sts and purl all purl sts.
Row 6—P5, BC, p1, SBC, k2, SFC, p1, FC, p5.
Row 8—P3, BC, p2, SBC, p1, k2, p1, SFC, p2, FC, p3.
Row 10—P3, k2, p3, SBC, p2, k2, p2, SFC, p3, k2, p3.
Row 12—P3, FC, SBC, p3, k2, p3, SFC, BC, p3.
Row 14—P5, BKC, p1, k2, p1, FKC, p5.
Row 16—P3, BC, FC, p2, k2, p2, BC, FC, p3.
Row 18—P3, k2, p4, FC, k2, BC, p4, k2, p3.
Row 20—P3, FC, p4, FKC, k2, p4, BC, p3.
Row 22—P5, FC, p2, k2, BKC, p2, BC, p5.
Row 24—P7, FC, FKC, k2, BC, p7.

Repeat Rows 1–24.

LEFT: *Hartshorn Cable*
RIGHT: *Double-Wrapped Braid*

Double-Wrapped Braid

Panel of 22 sts.

NOTES: FC, FKC, BC, and BKC—same as for Hartshorn Cable.

Rows 1 and 3 (Wrong side)—K5, p4, k8, p2, k3.
Row 2—P3, k2, p8, k4, p5.
Row 4—P3, FC, p6, FKC, p5.
Row 5 and all other wrong-side rows—Knit all knit sts and purl all purl sts.
Row 6—P5, FC, p2, BC, FC, p3.
Row 8—P7, k2, BC, p4, k2, p3.
Row 10—P7, BKC, p4, BC, p3.
Row 12—P5, BC, FC, BC, p5.
Row 14—P3, BC, p4, FKC, p7.

49

Row 16—P3, k2, p4, BC, k2, p7.
Row 18—P3, FC, BC, p2, FC, p5.
Row 20—P5, BKC, p6, FC, p3.
Row 22—P5, k4, p8, k2, p3.
Row 24—P5, BKC, p6, BC, p3.
Row 26—P3, BC, FC, p2, BC, p5.
Row 28—P3, k2, p4, FC, k2, p7.
Row 30—P3, FC, p4, FKC, p7.
Row 32—P5, FC, BC, FC, p5.
Row 34—P7, BKC, p4, FC, p3.
Row 36—P7, k2, FC, p4, k2, p3.
Row 38—P5, BC, p2, FC, BC, p3.
Row 40—P3, BC, p6, FKC, p5.

Repeat Rows 1–40.

Triplet Cable

CENTER PANEL: *Triplet Cable*
LEFT SIDE PANEL: *Cork Cable, Back Cross*
RIGHT SIDE PANEL: *Cork Cable, Front Cross*

In this beautiful design, three bobbles stand atop three ribs in the center of a fancy half-diamond, each motif opening out gracefully into the one above it. Notice the unusual use of cabled ribbing in the border, and of garter stitch for the central background.

Panel of 21 sts.

NOTES: Front Cross (FC): sl 3 sts to dpn and hold in front, k1, then k1-b, p1, k1-b from dpn.

Back Cross (BC): sl 1 st to dpn and hold in back, k1-b, p1, k1-b, then k1 from dpn.

Make Bobble (MB) as follows: (k1, yo, k1, yo, k1) in the same st, turn and p5, turn and k3, k2 tog, then pass the 3 knit sts one at a time over the last k2-tog st, completing bobble.

Row 1 (Wrong side)—K7, p1, k1, p3, k1, p1, k7.
Row 2—P6, BC, k1-b, FC, p6.
Row 3—K6, (p1, k1) 4 times, p1, k6.
Row 4—P5, BC, k1, k1-b, k1, FC, p5.
Row 5—K5, p1, k1, (p1, k2) twice, p1, k1, p1, k5.
Row 6—P4, BC, k2, k1-b, k2, FC, p4.
Row 7—K4, p1, k1, p2, k2, p1, k2, p2, k1, p1, k4.
Row 8—P3, BC, (k1-b, k2) twice, k1-b, FC, p3.
Row 9—K3, (p1, k1) twice, (p1, k2) twice, (p1, k1) twice, p1, k3.
Row 10—P2, BC, k1, (k1-b, k2) twice, k1-b, k1, FC, p2.

50

Row 11—K2, p1, k1, (p1, k2) 4 times, p1, k1, p1, k2.

Row 12—P1, BC, (k2, k1-b) 3 times, k2, FC, p1.

Row 13—(K1, p1) twice, k3, (p1, k2) twice, p1, k3, (p1, k1) twice.

Row 14—(P1, k1-b) twice, k3, (MB, k2) twice, MB, k3, (k1-b, p1) twice.

Row 15—(K1, p1) twice, k3, (p1-b, k2) twice, p1-b, k3, (p1, k1) twice.

Row 16—(P1, k1-b) twice, p3, k1-b, p1, k3-b, p1, k1-b, p3, (k1-b, p1) twice.

Repeat Rows 1–16.

Cork Cable

Here is a simple but interesting Irish cable design featuring three ribs crossing either to the left or to the right. The two types can be used to balance each other as shown. For a third variation, the cable can be worked in braided fashion by using the front cross (Version II, Row 6) on the sixth row and the back cross (Version I, Row 6) on the twelfth.

Panel of 14 sts.

VERSION I. BACK CROSS

Row 1 (Wrong side) and all other wrong-side rows—K2, (p2, k2) 3 times.

Rows 2, 4, 8, and 10—P2, (k2, p2) 3 times.

Row 6—P2, k2, p2, Back Cross the next 6 sts as follows: sl 4 sts to dpn and hold in back, k2, then sl the 2 purl sts back to left-hand needle and purl them; then k2 from dpn; p2.

Row 12—P2, Back Cross the next 6 sts as in Row 6; p2, k2, p2.

Repeat Rows 1–12.

VERSION II. FRONT CROSS

Work the same as I, above, with the following exceptions:

Row 6—P2, Front Cross the next 6 sts as follows: sl 4 sts to dpn and hold in front, k2, then sl the 2 purl sts back to left-hand needle and purl them; then k2 from dpn; p2, k2, p2.

Row 12—P2, k2, p2, Front Cross the next 6 sts as in Row 6; p2.

Repeat Rows 1–12.

51

Aran Diamond and Bobble

Panel of 17 sts.

NOTES: Front Cross (FC)—sl 2 sts to dpn and hold in front, p1, then k2 from dpn.

Back Cross (BC)—sl 1 st to dpn and hold in back, k2, then p1 from dpn.

Rows 1 and 3 (Wrong side)—K6, p2, k1, p2, k6.

Row 2—P6, sl next 3 sts to dpn and hold in back, k2, then sl the purl st from dpn back to left-hand needle and purl it, then k2 from dpn; p6.

Row 4—P5, BC, k1, FC, p5.

Row 5 and all subsequent wrong-side rows—Knit all knit sts and purl all purl sts.

Row 6—P4, BC, k1, p1, k1, FC, p4.

Row 8—P3, BC, (k1, p1) twice, k1, FC, p3.

Row 10—P2, BC, (k1, p1) 3 times, k1, FC, p2.

Row 12—P2, FC, (p1, k1) 3 times, p1, BC, p2.

Row 14—P3, FC, (p1, k1) twice, p1, BC, p3.

Row 16—P4, FC, p1, k1, p1, BC, p4.

Row 18—P5, FC, p1, BC, p5.

Row 20—Repeat Row 2.

Row 22—P5, BC, p1, FC, p5.

Row 24—P4, BC, p3, FC, p4.

Row 26—P4, k2, p2, Make Bobble as follows: (k1, yo, k1, yo, k1) in next st, turn and p5, turn and k5, turn and p2 tog, p1, p2 tog, turn and sl 1—k2 tog—psso, completing Bobble; p2, k2, p4.

Row 28—P4, FC, p3, BC, p4.

Row 30—Repeat Row 18.

Repeat Rows 1–30.

LEFT: *Aran Diamond and Bobble*
CENTER: *Clustered Braid*
RIGHT: *Cluster Cable*

Clustered Braid

Panel of 20 sts.

NOTES: FC and BC—same as for Aran Diamond and Bobble.

Back Knit Cross (BKC)—sl 2 sts to dpn and hold in back, k2, then k2 from dpn.

Rows 1 and 3 (Wrong side)—K4, (p4, k4) twice.

Row 2—P4, BKC, p4, sl next 2 sts to dpn and hold in front, k2, then k2 from dpn; p4.

Row 4—P3, BC, FC, p2, BC, FC, p3.

Row 5 and all subsequent wrong-side rows—Knit all knit sts and
  purl all purl sts.

Row 6—P2, (BC, p2, FC) twice, p2.

Row 8—P2, k2, p4, BKC, p4, k2, p2.

Row 10—P2, k2, p4, k4, p4, k2, p2.

Row 12—Repeat Row 8.

Row 14—P2, (FC, p2, BC) twice, p2.

Row 16—P3, FC, BC, p2, FC, BC, p3.

Rows 18 and 20—Repeat Rows 2 and 4.

Row 22—P3, (k2, p2) twice, k2; then sl the last 6 sts worked onto
  dpn and wrap yarn 4 times counterclockwise around these 6
  sts; then sl the 6 sts back to right-hand needle; p2, k2, p3.

Row 24—Repeat Row 16.

Repeat Rows 1–24.

Cluster Cable

Panel of 16 sts.

NOTES: FC, BC, and BKC—same as for Clustered Braid.

Single Front Cross (SFC)—sl 1 st to dpn and hold in front,
p1, then k1 from dpn.

Single Back Cross (SBC)—sl 1 st to dpn and hold in back, k1,
then p1 from dpn.

Rows 1 and 3 (Wrong side)—K6, p4, k6.

Row 2—P6, BKC, p6.

Row 4—P5, BC, FC, p5.

Row 5 and all subsequent wrong-side rows—Knit all knit sts and
  purl all purl sts.

Row 6—P4, BC, p2, FC, p4.

Row 8—P4, RT, p4, LT, p4.

Row 10—P3, SBC, SFC, p2, SBC, SFC, p3.

Row 12—P2, (SBC, p2, SFC) twice, p2.

Row 14—P2, k1, p4, k2; then sl the last 2 sts worked onto dpn
  and wrap yarn 6 times counterclockwise around these 2 sts; then
  sl the 2 sts back to right-hand needle; p4, k1, p2.

Row 16—P2, (SFC, p2, SBC) twice, p2.

Row 18—P3, SFC, SBC, p2, SFC, SBC, p3.

Row 20—P4, LT, p4, RT, p4.

Row 22—P4, FC, p2, BC, p4.

Row 24—P5, FC, BC, p5.

Repeat Rows 1–24.

Spanish Tile Cable
LEFT: *Front Cross*
RIGHT: *Back Cross*

Spanish Tile Cable

Contributed by Ruth S. Stein, Los Angeles, California

A diamond with a few novel touches, this large, commanding cable is ideal as a central motif in a fancy sweater or jacket. One repeat is handsome on the back of a mitten or glove. Note the small difference between the Front Cross and Back Cross versions.

Panel of 22 sts.

NOTES: Front Cross (FC): sl 3 sts to dpn and hold in front, k3, then k3 from dpn.

Back Cross (BC): sl 3 sts to dpn and hold in back, k3, then k3 from dpn.

Front Purl Cross (FPC): sl 3 sts to dpn and hold in front, p3, then k3 from dpn.

Back Purl Cross (BPC): sl 3 sts to dpn and hold in back, k3, then p3 from dpn.

Rows 1, 3, and 5 (Wrong side)—K8, p6, k8.
Rows 2 and 4—P8, k6, p8.
Row 6—P5, k3, FC, (or BC), k3, p5.
Rows 7, 9, and 11—K5, p12, k5.
Rows 8 and 10—P5, k12, p5.
Row 12—P2, k3, BPC, FPC, k3, p2.
Rows 13, 15, and 17—K2, p6, k6, p6, k2.
Rows 14 and 16—P2, k6, p6, k6, p2.
Row 18—P2, BPC, p6, FPC, p2.
Rows 19, 21, and 23—K2, p3, k12, p3, k2.
Rows 20 and 22—P2, k3, p12, k3, p2.
Row 24—P2, FC, p6, BC, p2.
Rows 25 through 29—Repeat Rows 13 through 17.
Row 30—P5, FC, BC, p5.
Rows 31 through 35—Repeat Rows 7 through 11.
Row 36—P8, FC (or BC), p8.

Repeat Rows 1–36.

CENTER PANEL: *Counter-Twisted Oval*
SIDE PANELS: *Twin Waves*

Counter-Twisted Oval

This graceful design develops from a small simple cable, which is twisted right, left, and right in the center.

Panel of 26 sts.

NOTES: Front Cross (FC)—sl 2 sts to dpn and hold in front, p2, then k2 from dpn.

Front Knit Cross (FKC)—Same as Front Cross, but *knit* all sts.

Single Front Cross (SFC)—sl 2 sts to dpn and hold in front, p1, then k2 from dpn.

Back Cross (BC)—sl 2 sts to dpn and hold in back, k2, then p2 from dpn.

Back Knit Cross (BKC)—Same as Back Cross, but *knit* all sts.

Single Back Cross (SBC)—sl 1 st to dpn and hold in back, k2, then p1 from dpn.

Rows 1 and 3 (Wrong side)—K11, p4, k11.

Row 2—P11, BKC, p11.

Row 4—P9, BKC, FKC, p9.

Row 5 and all subsequent wrong-side rows—Knit all knit sts and purl all purl sts.

Row 6—P7, BC, FKC, FC, p7.

Row 8—P5, BC, p2, k4, p2, FC, p5.

Row 10—P4, SBC, p4, FKC, p4, SFC, p4.

Row 12—P3, SBC, p3, BKC, FKC, p3, SFC, p3.

Row 14—P2, SBC, p2, BC, k4, FC, p2, SFC, p2.

Row 16—P2, k2, p1, BC, p2, BKC, p2, FC, p1, k2, p2.

Row 18—P2, k2, p1, k2, p4, k4, p4, k2, p1, k2, p2.

Row 20—P2, k2, p1, FC, p2, BKC, p2, BC, p1, k2, p2.

Row 22—P2, SFC, p2, FC, k4, BC, p2, SBC, p2.

Row 24—P3, SFC, p3, FC, BC, p3, SBC, p3.

Row 26—P4, SFC, p4, FKC, p4, SBC, p4.

Row 28—P5, FC, p2, k4, p2, BC, p5.

Row 30—P7, FC, FKC, BC, p7.

Row 32—P9, FC, BC, p9.

Repeat Rows 1–32.

Twin Waves

To arrange this cable in opposition panels as shown, in *one* of the panels work FKC instead of BKC in Rows 2 and 12. Begin one cable with Row 1, the other with Row 11.

Panel of 15 sts.

NOTES: FC, FKC, SFC, BC, BKC, and SBC—Same as for Counter-Twisted Oval.

Rows 1 and 3 (Wrong side)—K3, p4, k4, p2, k2.

Row 2—P2, k2, p4, BKC, p3.

Row 4—P2, FC, BC, k2, p3.

Row 5 and all subsequent wrong-side rows—Knit all knit sts and purl all purl sts.

Row 6—P4, BC, p1, SBC, p3.

Row 8—P3, SBC, p1, BKC, p4.

Row 10—P3, k2, BC, FC, p2.

Row 12—P3, BKC, p4, k2, p2.

Row 14—P3, k2, FC, BC, p2.

Row 16—P3, SFC, p1, FC, p4.

Row 18—P4, FKC, p1, SFC, p3.

Row 20—P2, BC, FC, k2, p3.

Repeat Rows 1–20.

Cam Cable

Here is a marvelously unusual cable for your most "original" fisherman sweaters. The big five-stitch rib is shredded into five separate ribs, in a diagonal ladder-like design. Notice that there is no actual crossing (5 over 5) of the large ribs, as this would squeeze the pattern too much. Instead, an illusion of a cable twist is cleverly achieved by means of increases and decreases.

CENTER PANEL: *Cam Cable*
SIDE PANELS: *Slack Line, or Drunken-Sailor Cable*

Panel of 20 sts.

NOTES: Front Cross (FC): sl 1 st to dpn and hold in front, p1, then k1 from dpn.

Double Front Cross (2FC): sl 2 sts to dpn and hold in front, p1, then k2 from dpn.

Triple Front Cross (3FC): sl 3 sts to dpn and hold in front, p1, then k3 from dpn.

Back Cross (BC): sl 1 st to dpn and hold in back, k1, then p1 from dpn.

Increase (inc): purl into the front and back of the same st.

Rows 1 and 3 (Wrong side)—K4, p5, k2, p5, k4.
Row 2—P4, k5, p2, k5, p4.
Row 4—P3, inc, k4, ssk, k2 tog, k4, inc, p3.
Row 5—K5, p10, k5.
Row 6—P4, BC, * sl next 4 sts to dpn and hold in front, p1, then k4 from dpn; k2 tog *, k2, inc, p4.
Row 7—K6, p7, k2, p1, k4.
Row 8—P3, BC, p2, rep from * to * of Row 6, inc, p5.
Row 9—K7, p5, k4, p1, k3.
Row 10—P2, BC, p3, BC, 3FC, p7.
Row 11—K7, p3, k2, p1, k4, p1, k2.
Row 12—P2, FC, p2, BC, p2, 3FC, p6.
Row 13—K6, p3, k4, p1, k2, p1, k3.
Row 14—P3, FC, BC, p3, BC, 2FC, p5.
Row 15—K5, p2, k2, p1, k4, p2, k4.
Row 16—P4, 2FC, p2, BC, p2, 2FC, p4.
Row 17—K4, p2, k4, p1, k2, p2, k5.
Row 18—P5, 2FC, BC, p3, BC, FC, p3.
Row 19—K3, p1, k2, p1, k4, p3, k6.
Row 20—P6, 3FC, p2, BC, p2, FC, p2.
Row 21—K2, p1, k4, p1, k2, p3, k7.
Row 22—P7, work 3FC but *knit* all sts, BC, p3, BC, p2.
Row 23—K3, p1, k4, p5, k7.
Row 24—P5, p2 tog, k1, * sl next 4 sts to dpn and hold in front, knit into front and back of next st, then k4 from dpn *, p2, BC, p3.
Row 25—K4, p1, k2, p7, k6.
Row 26—P4, p2 tog, k3, rep from * to * of Row 24, BC, p4.
Row 27—Repeat Row 5.

Row 28—P3, p2 tog, k5, purl into front and back of the running thread between the st just worked and the next st; k5, p2 tog, p3.

Repeat Rows 1–28.

Slack Line, or
Drunken-Sailor Cable

This pattern is fun, easy to work, and mysterious—everyone wonders how the cable is made to slither gently from side to side! It is done with increases and decreases on every 4th row. Notice that the cable is twisted to the right when traveling to the left, and to the left when traveling to the right. This makes it seem about to untwist itself, and adds to the "precarious" effect.

Panel of 12 sts.

NOTES: Front Cross (FC): sl 2 sts to dpn and hold in front, k2, then k2 from dpn.

Back Cross (BC): sl 2 sts to dpn and hold in back, k2, then k2 from dpn.

Increase (inc): Purl into the front and back of the same st.

Rows 1, 3, and 5 (Wrong side)—K2, p4, k6.
Row 2—P6, k4, p2.
Row 4—P6, FC, p2.
Row 6—P4, p2 tog, k4, inc, p1.
Row 7 and all subsequent wrong-side rows—Knit all knit and increase sts, purl all purl sts.
Row 8—P5, FC, p3.
Row 10—P3, p2 tog, k4, inc, p2.
Row 12—P4, FC, p4.
Row 14—P2, p2 tog, k4, inc, p3.
Row 16—P3, FC, p5.
Row 18—P1, p2 tog, k4, inc, p4.
Row 20—P2, FC, p6.
Row 22—P2, k4, p6.
Row 24—P2, BC, p6.
Row 26—P1, inc, k4, p2 tog, p4.
Row 28—P3, BC, p5.
Row 30—P2, inc, k4, p2 tog, p3.
Row 32—P4, BC, p4.
Row 34—P3, inc, k4, p2 tog, p2.
Row 36—P5, BC, p3.
Row 38—P4, inc, k4, p2 tog, p1.
Row 40—P6, BC, p2.

Repeat Rows 1–40.

Homes of Donegal

In the classic Aran tradition, this pattern clusters four greatly enlarged popcorn motifs—which really become bell motifs as a result—inside an embossed diamond. The same idea is often seen in an expanded form with larger diamonds containing five, seven or nine motifs.

LEFT: *Homes of Donegal*
RIGHT: *Spearhead and Chain*

Panel of 19 sts.

NOTES: BC (Back Cross): sl 1 st to dpn and hold in back, k2, then p1 from dpn.

FC (Front Cross): sl 2 sts to dpn and hold in front, p1, then k2 from dpn.

Rows 1 and 3 (Wrong side)—K7, p2, k1, p2, k7.

Row 2—P7, sl next 3 sts to dpn and hold in back, k2, sl the purl st from dpn back to left-hand needle and purl it, then k2 from dpn; p7.

Row 4—P6, BC, p1, FC, p6.

Row 5—K6, p2, k3, p2, k6.

Row 6—P5, BC, p1, (k1, yo, k1, yo, k1) in next st, p1, FC, p5.

Row 7—K5, p2, k2, p5, k2, p2, k5.

Row 8—P4, BC, p2, k5, p2, FC, p4.

Row 9—K4, p2, k3, p5, k3, p2, k4.

Row 10—P3, BC, p3, ssk, k1, k2 tog, p3, FC, p3.

Row 11—K3, p2, k4, p3, k4, p2, k3.

Row 12—P2, BC, p1, (k1, yo, k1, yo, k1) in next st, p2, sl 1—k2 tog—psso, p2, (k1, yo, k1, yo, k1) in next st, p1, FC, p2.

Row 13—K2, p2, k2, p5, k2, p1, k2, p5, k2, p2, k2.

Row 14—P1, BC, p2, k5, p5, k5, p2, FC, p1.

Row 15—K1, p2, k3, p5, k5, p5, k3, p2, k1.

Row 16—P1, FC, p2, ssk, k1, k2 tog, p5, ssk, k1, k2 tog, p2, BC, p1.

Row 17—K2, p2, k2, p3, k5, p3, k2, p2, k2.

Row 18—P2, FC, p1, sl 1—k2 tog—psso, p2, (k1, yo, k1, yo, k1) in next st, p2, sl 1—k2 tog—psso, p1, BC, p2.

Row 19—K3, p2, k1, p1, k2, p5, k2, p1, k1, p2, k3.

Row 20—P3, FC, p3, k5, p3, BC, p3.

Row 21—K4, p2, k3, p5, k3, p2, k4.

Row 22—P4, FC, p2, ssk, k1, k2 tog, p2, BC, p4.

Row 23—K5, p2, k2, p3, k2, p2, k5.

Row 24—P5, FC, p1, sl 1—k2 tog—psso, p1, BC, p5.

Row 25—K6, p2, k1, p1, k1, p2, k6.

Row 26—P6, FC, p1, BC, p6.

Repeat Rows 1–26.

Spearhead and Chain

The salty Aran Isles breathed a true flavor of the sea into this cable, inspired by the harpoon with attached chain or twisted rope. Slight variations on the stylized design create the more gentle Valentine Cable (See p. 23).

Panel of 26 sts.

NOTES: BC (Back Cross): sl 1 st to dpn and hold in back, k2, then p1 from dpn

BKC (Back Knit Cross): sl 2 sts to dpn and hold in back, k2, then k2 from dpn.

FC (Front Cross): sl 2 sts to dpn and hold in front, p1, then k2 from dpn.

SBC (Single Back Cross): sl 1 st to dpn and hold in back, k1, then p1 from dpn.

SBKC (Single Back Knit Cross): Same as SBC, but knit both sts.

SFC (Single Front Cross): sl 1 st to dpn and hold in front, p1, then k1 from dpn.

SFKC (Single Front Knit Cross): Same as SFC, but knit both sts.

Row 1 (Wrong side)—(K2, p1) twice, k5, p4, k5, (p1, k2) twice.
Row 2—P2, SFC, SBC, p5, BKC, p5, SFC, SBC, p2.
Row 3—K3, p2, k6, p4, k6, p2, k3.
Row 4—P3, SBKC, p5, BC, FC, p5, SFKC, p3.
Row 5—K3, p2, k5, p2, k2, p2, k5, p2, k3.
Row 6—P2, SBC, SFC, p3, BC, p2, FC, p3, SBC, SFC, p2.
Row 7—(K2, p1) twice, k3, (p2, k1) twice, p2, k3, (p1, k2) twice.
Row 8—(P2, k1) twice, p2, BC, k4, FC, p2, (k1, p2) twice.
Row 9—(K2, p1) twice, k2, p2, k1, p4, k1, p2, k2, (p1, k2) twice.
Row 10—P2, SFC, SBC, p1, BC, p1, BKC, p1, FC, p1, SFC, SBC, p2.
Row 11—K3, (p2, k2) twice, p4, (k2, p2) twice, k3.
Row 12—P3, SBKC, (p1, BC) twice, (FC, p1) twice, SFKC, p3.
Row 13—K6, (p2, k2) 3 times, p2, k6.
Row 14—P5, (BC, p1) twice, (p1, FC) twice, p5.
Row 15—K5, p2, k2, p2, k4, p2, k2, p2, k5.
Row 16—P4, BC, p1, BC, p4, FC, p1, FC, p4.
Row 17—K4, p2, k2, p2, k6, p2, k2, p2, k4.
Row 18—P3, BC, p2, FC, p4, BC, p2, FC, p3.
Row 19—K3, (p2, k4) 3 times, p2, k3.
Row 20—P2, SBC, SFC, p3, FC, p2, BC, p3, SBC, SFC, p2.
Row 21—(K2, p1) twice, k4, p2, k2, p2, k4, (p1, k2) twice.
Row 22—(P2, k1) twice, p4, FC, BC, p4, (k1, p2) twice.

Repeat Rows 1–22.

Latticed Diamond

CENTER PANEL: *Latticed Diamond*
SIDE PANELS: *Riptide Wave*

In this beautiful cable, the three stitches forming the diamond borders are separated from each other, one at a time, to form the interior design of single knit stitches; then they re-join each other in the upper half of the diamond. Therefore there are three types of front cross and three types of back cross involved in working the pattern, but they differ only in the number of knit stitches used.

Panel of 22 sts.

NOTES: Single Front Cross (1FC)—sl 1 st to dpn and hold in front, p1, then k1 from dpn.

Double Front Cross (2FC)—sl 2 sts to dpn and hold in front, p1, then k2 from dpn.

Triple Front Cross (3FC)—sl 3 sts to dpn and hold in front, p1, then k3 from dpn.

Single Back Cross (1BC)—sl 1 st to dpn and hold in back, k1, then p1 from dpn.

Double Back Cross (2BC)—sl 1 st to dpn and hold in back, k2, then p1 from dpn.

Triple Back Cross (3BC)—sl 1 st to dpn and hold in back, k3, then p1 from dpn.

Rows 1 and 3 (Wrong side)—K8, p6, k8.

Row 2—P8, sl next 3 sts to dpn and hold in back, k3, then k3 from dpn, p8.

Row 4—P7, 3BC, 3FC, p7.

Row 5 and all subsequent wrong-side rows *except* Rows 13, 17, and 21—Knit all knit sts and purl all purl sts.

Row 6—P6, 3BC, p2, 3FC, p6.

Row 8—P5, 2BC, k1, p4, k1, 2FC, p5.

Row 10—P4, 2BC, p1, 1FC, p2, 1BC, p1, 2FC, p4.

Row 12—P3, 1BC, k1, p3, 1FC, 1BC, p3, k1, 1FC, p3.

Row 13—K3, p1, k1, p1, k4, sl next st to dpn and hold in front, p1, then p1 from dpn; k4, p1, k1, p1, k3.

Row 14—P2, 1BC, p1, 1FC, p2, 1BC, 1FC, p2, 1BC, p1, 1FC, p2.

Row 16—P2, k1, p3, 1FC, 1BC, p2, 1FC, 1BC, p3, k1, p2.

Row 17—K2, p1, (k4, sl next st to dpn and hold in back, p1, then p1 from dpn) twice, k4, p1, k2.

Row 18—P2, k1, p3, 1BC, 1FC, p2, 1BC, 1FC, p3, k1, p2.

Row 20—P2, 1FC, p1, 1BC, p2, 1FC, 1BC, p2, 1FC, p1, 1BC, p2.

Row 21—Repeat Row 13.

Row 22—P3, 1FC, k1, p3, 1BC, 1FC, p3, k1, 1BC, p3.

Row 24—P4, 2FC, p1, 1BC, p2, 1FC, p1, 2BC, p4.

Row 26—P5, 2FC, k1, p4, k1, 2BC, p5.

Row 28—P6, 3FC, p2, 3BC, p6.

Row 30—P7, 3FC, 3BC, p7.

Repeat Rows 1–30.

Riptide Wave

Panel of 12 sts.

NOTES: 1FC, 2FC, 3FC, 1BC, 2BC, and 3BC—Same as for Latticed Diamond.

Row 1 (Wrong side)—K4, p3, k5.
Row 2—P4, 3BC, p4.
Row 3 and all subsequent wrong-side rows—Knit all knit sts and purl all purl sts.
Row 4—P3, 2BC, 1FC, p4.
Row 6—P2, 2BC, p2, 1FC, p3.
Row 8—P1, 2BC, p4, 1FC, p2.
Row 10—P1, 2FC, p4, 1BC, p2.
Row 12—P2, 2FC, p2, 1BC, p3.
Row 14—P3, 2FC, 1BC, p4.
Row 16—P4, 3FC, p4.
Row 18—P4, 1BC, 2FC, p3.
Row 20—P3, 1BC, p2, 2FC, p2.
Row 22—P2, 1BC, p4, 2FC, p1.
Row 24—P2, 1FC, p4, 2BC, p1.
Row 26—P3, 1FC, p2, 2BC, p2.
Row 28—P4, 1FC, 2BC, p3.

Repeat Rows 1–28.

Three Cables with Irish Knots: Hollow Oak, Crazy Maypole, and Lorgnette Cable

LEFT: *Hollow Oak*
CENTER: *Crazy Maypole*
RIGHT: *Lorgnette Cable*

Though these three cables are quite diverse in appearance, all three are decorated with Irish Knots, single or in clusters. Hollow Oak and Lorgnette Cable are fairly straightforward patterns, with no tricks about them except their own special brand of novelty. But the knitter who uses Crazy Maypole must watch what she is doing. It is an off-center, free-swinging sort of pattern incorporating knots, twists, and an "inside-out" cable cross in which one knit stitch is crossed in front of two purl stitches—the reverse of the usual system. In spite of its apparent eccentricity, the Maypole is a highly disciplined design, consistent with its own internal symmetry; the second half of the pattern is the exact opposite, in every detail, of the first half.

NOTE FOR ALL THREE PATTERNS: Make Knot (MK) as follows—(k1, p1, k1, p1, k1, p1, k1) in one stitch, making 7 sts from 1; then with point of left-hand needle pass the 2nd, 3rd, 4th, 5th, 6th, and 7th sts on right-hand needle separately over the last st made, completing Knot.

I. HOLLOW OAK

Panel of 15 sts.

NOTES: Front Cross (FC)—sl 2 sts to dpn and hold in front, p1, then k2 from dpn.

Back Cross (BC)—sl 1 st to dpn and hold in back, k2, then p1 from dpn.

Rows 1, 3, 5, and 7 (Wrong side)—K5, p5, k5.
Row 2—P5, k2, MK, k2, p5.
Row 4—P5, MK, k3, MK, p5.
Row 6—Repeat Row 2.
Row 8—P4, BC, p1, FC, p4.
Row 9—K4, p2, k1, p1, k1, p2, k4.
Row 10—P3, BC, k1, p1, k1, FC, p3.
Row 11—K3, p3, k1, p1, k1, p3, k3.
Row 12—P2, BC, (p1, k1) twice, p1, FC, p2.
Row 13—K2, p2, (k1, p1) 3 times, k1, p2, k2.
Row 14—P2, k3, (p1, k1) twice, p1, k3, p2.
Rows 15, 17, and 19—Repeat Rows 13, 11, and 9.
Row 16—P2, FC, (p1, k1) twice, p1, BC, p2.
Row 18—P3, FC, k1, p1, k1, BC, p3.
Row 20—P4, FC, p1, BC, p4.

Repeat Rows 1–20.

II. CRAZY MAYPOLE

Panel of 18 sts.

NOTES: Front Cross (FC)—sl 1 st to dpn and hold in front, p2, then k1 from dpn.

Back Cross (BC)—sl 2 sts to dpn and hold in back, k1, then p2 from dpn.

Row 1 (Wrong side)—K9, p1, k2, p1, k5.
Row 2—P5, k1-b, p2, k1-b, p3, MK, p5.
Row 3—K5, p1, k3, p1, k2, p1, k5.
Row 4—P2, MK, p2, LT, p1, k1-b, p3, k1-b, p5.
Row 5—K5, p1, k3, p1, k1, p1, k3, p1, k2.
Row 6—P2, FC, p1, LT, k1-b, p1, BC, p2, MK, p2.
Row 7—K2, p1, k4, p1, k1, p2, k2, p1, k4.

Row 8—P4, FC, LT, RT, p2, BC, p2.
Row 9—K4, p1, k3, p2, k1, p1, k6.
Row 10—P6, LT, RT, p1, BC, p4.
Row 11—K6, p1, k2, p2, k7.
Row 12—P7, LT, BC, p6.
Row 13—K8, p3, k7.
Row 14—P7, FC, p2, MK, p5.
Row 15—K5, p1, k2, p1, k9.
Row 16—P5, MK, p3, k1-b, p2, k1-b, p5.
Row 17—K5, p1, k2, p1, k3, p1, k5.
Row 18—P5, k1-b, p3, k1-b, p1, RT, p2, MK, p2.
Row 19—K2, p1, k3, p1, k1, p1, k3, p1, k5.
Row 20—P2, MK, p2, FC, p1, k1-b, RT, p1, BC, p2.
Row 21—K4, p1, k2, p2, k1, p1, k4, p1, k2.
Row 22—P2, FC, p2, LT, RT, BC, p4.
Row 23—K6, p1, k1, p2, k3, p1, k4.
Row 24—P4, FC, p1, LT, RT, p6.
Row 25—K7, p2, k2, p1, k6.
Row 26—P6, FC, RT, p7.
Row 27—K7, p3, k8.
Row 28—P5, MK, p2, BC, p7.

Repeat Rows 1–28.

III. LORGNETTE CABLE

Panel of 12 sts.

NOTES: Front Cross (FC)—sl 2 sts to dpn and hold in front, p2, then k2 from dpn.

Back Cross (BC)—sl 2 sts to dpn and hold in back, k2, then p2 from dpn.

Single Front Cross (SFC)—sl 2 sts to dpn and hold in front, p1, then k2 from dpn.

Single Back Cross (SBC)—sl 1 st to dpn and hold in back, k2, then p1 from dpn.

Rows 1 and 3 (Wrong side)—K2, p2, k4, p2, k2.
Row 2—P2, k2, p4, k2, p2.
Row 4—P2, FC, BC, p2.
Row 5—K4, p4, k4.
Row 6—P1, FC, p4.
Row 7—K4, p2, k6.
Row 8—P6, SFC, p3.
Row 9—K3, p2, k7.
Row 10—P7, SFC, p2.
Row 11—K2, p2, k8.
Row 12—P3, MK, p4, k2, p2.

Rows 13, 15, 17, and 19—Repeat Rows 11, 9, 7, and 5.
Row 14—P7, SBC, p2.
Row 16—P6, SBC, p3.
Row 18—P4, work BC but *knit* all 4 sts; p4.
Row 20—P2, BC, FC, p2.
Rows 21, 22, 23, 24, and 25—Repeat Rows 1, 2, 3, 4, and 5.
Row 26—P4, BC, p4.
Row 27—K6, p2, k4.
Row 28—P3, SBC, p6.
Row 29—K7, p2, k3.
Row 30—P2, SBC, p7.
Row 31—K8, p2, k2.
Row 32—P2, k2, p4, MK, p3.
Rows 33, 35, 37, and 39—Repeat Rows 31, 29, 27, and 5.
Row 34—P2, SFC, p7.
Row 36—P3, SFC, p6.
Row 38—P4, work FC but *knit* all 4 sts; p4.
Row 40—Repeat Row 20.

Repeat Rows 1–40.

LEFT: *Alternating Cable*
RIGHT: *Aran Braid*

Alternating Cable

This pattern is definitely "different". It is really a double cable, but worked alternately to the right and left so that the two sides do not correspond. The cable is simple to work.

Panel of 12 sts.

Row 1 (Wrong side) and all other wrong-side rows—K2, p8, k2.
Row 2—P2, k4, sl 2 sts to dpn and hold in front, k2, then k2 from dpn; p2.
Row 4—P2, k8, p2.
Row 6—Repeat Row 2.
Row 8—P2, sl 2 sts to dpn and hold in back, k2, then k2 from dpn; k4, p2.
Row 10—Repeat Row 4.
Row 12—Repeat Row 8.

Repeat Rows 1–12.

Aran Braid

With this easy pattern, even a beginner can make thick, fancy, intricate-looking cables to decorate hats, mittens, jackets, or outdoor sweaters. The pattern appears to be very carefully plaited, but in fact its four simple rows can be worked with a minimum of concentration.

Panel of 12 sts.

Rows 1 and 3 (Wrong side)—K2, p8, k2.

Row 2—P2, (sl 2 sts to dpn and hold in back, k2, then k2 from dpn) twice, p2.

Row 4—P2, k2, sl 2 sts to dpn and hold in front, k2, then k2 from dpn; k2, p2.

Repeat Rows 1–4.

Disc Cables

Contributed by Hildegard M. Elsner, Aldan, Pennsylvania

A circular shape is not common in knitting patterns, because knitting simply does not lend itself to the construction of such a shape. Knit and purl stitches, their angles and their methods of formation, are much better suited to vertical, horizontal, and diagonal designs. However, in these three cables—Banjo Cable, Dollar Cable, and Seed Wishbone—we see one of the few ways of making round shapes in knitting.

I. BANJO CABLE

Panel of 12 sts.

Row 1 (Wrong side)—K4, p4, k4.

Row 2—P4, k4, p4.

Row 3—K4, p1, sl 2 wyif, p1, k4.

Row 4—P2, sl next 3 sts to dpn and hold in back, k1, then p1, k1, p1 from dpn; sl next st to dpn and hold in front, k1, p1, k1, then k1 from dpn; p2.

Rows 5, 7, and 9—K2, (p1, k1) 3 times, p2, k2.

Rows 6, 8, and 10—P2, (k1, p1) 3 times, k2, p2.

Row 11—K2, sl 1 wyif, (k1, p1) 3 times, sl 1 wyif, k2.

Row 12—P2, sl next st to dpn and hold in front, p2, k1, then k1 from dpn; sl next 3 sts to dpn and hold in back, k1, then k1, p2 from dpn; p2.

Rows 13, 14, 15, and 16—Repeat Rows 1 and 2 twice.

Repeat Rows 1–16.

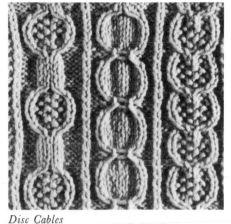

Disc Cables
LEFT: *Banjo Cable*
CENTER: *Dollar Cable*
RIGHT: *Seed Wishbone*

II. DOLLAR CABLE

Panel of 12 sts.

Row 1 (Wrong side)—K2, sl 1 wyif, p6, sl 1 wyif, k2.
Row 2—P2, sl next st to dpn and hold in front, p3, then k1 from dpn; sl next 3 sts to dpn and hold in back, k1, then p3 from dpn; p2.
Row 3—K5, p2, k5.
Row 4—P2, sl next 3 sts to dpn and hold in back, k1, then k3 from dpn; sl next st to dpn and hold in front, k3, then k1 from dpn; p2.
Rows 5, 7, and 9—K2, p8, k2.
Rows 6, 8, and 10—P2, k8, p2.

Repeat Rows 1–10.

III. SEED WISHBONE

Panel of 12 sts.

Row 1 (Right side)—P2, sl next 3 sts to dpn and hold in back, k1, then p1, k1, p1 from dpn; sl next st to dpn and hold in front, k1, p1, k1, then k1 from dpn; p2.
Rows 2, 4, and 6—K2, (p1, k1) 3 times, p2, k2.
Rows 3 and 5—P2, (k1, p1) 3 times, k2, p2.
Row 7—P2, k1, p1, k3, p1, k2, p2.
Row 8—K2, p1, k1, p3, k1, p2, k2.

Repeat Rows 1–8.

Five-Rib Braid Cables: Tight, Loose, and Elongated

Tight Five-Rib Braid is the basic cable here—similar to Aran Braid, but with five interlocking ribs instead of four. The other two Five-Rib braids are variations. All three are beautiful cables, not difficult to work but interesting.

I. TIGHT FIVE-RIB BRAID

This little cable is very dense and firm, crossing two stitches over two every other row.

Panel of 14 sts.

Notes: Front Cross (FC)—sl 2 sts to dpn and hold in front, k2, then k2 from dpn.

Back Cross (BC)—sl 2 sts to dpn and hold in back, k2, then k2 from dpn.

LEFT: *Tight Five-Rib Braid*
CENTER: *Loose Five-Rib Braid*
RIGHT: *Elongated Five-Rib Braid*

66

Rows 1 and 3 (Wrong side)—K2, p10, k2.
Row 2—P2, k2, (FC) twice, p2.
Row 4—P2, (BC) twice, k2, p2.

Repeat Rows 1–4.

II. LOOSE FIVE-RIB BRAID

This cable has the same form as Tight Five-Rib Braid, but two plain right side rows are inserted so that the pattern takes twice as many rows. Also, single purl stitches are placed between the ribs.

Panel of 18 sts:

NOTES: Front Cross (FC)—sl 3 sts to dpn and hold in front, k2, then sl the purl st from dpn back to left-hand needle and purl it, then k2 from dpn.

Back Cross (BC)—sl 3 sts to dpn and hold in back, k2, then sl the purl st from dpn back to left-hand needle and purl it, then k2 from dpn.

Row 1 (Wrong side) and all other wrong-side rows—K2, (p2, k1) 4 times, p2, k2.
Row 2—P2, (k2, p1) 4 times, k2, p2.
Row 4—P2, k2, (p1, FC) twice, p2.
Row 6—Repeat Row 2.
Row 8—P2, (BC, p1) twice, k2, p2.

Repeat Rows 1–8.

III. ELONGATED FIVE-RIB BRAID

One more plain row is included in this version, so that the pattern is elongated eccentrically, or half-way. Still another plain row could be inserted between Rows 6 and 8—making 12 rows in all—to form an even looser version. The wrong-side rows could be worked just like the wrong-side rows in the Loose Braid, but here they are purled, which makes a slight difference in the cabled crossings (see Notes).

Panel of 18 sts.

NOTES: FC and BC—same as for Loose Five-Rib Braid. The central stitch is not a purl stitch, since it is not knitted on the preceding row; nevertheless it is put back on the left-hand needle and purled in the same way.

Row 1 (Wrong side) and all other wrong-side rows—K2, p14, k2.
Rows 2, 4, 6, and 8—Same as Rows 2, 4, 6, and 8 of Loose Five-Rib Braid, above.
Row 10—Repeat Row 2.

Repeat Rows 1–10.

Rib and Purl Cable

Contributed by Marion C. Magnussen, Lake Mills, Wisconsin

Panel of 16 sts.

Rib and Purl Cable
LEFT: *Back Cross Version*
RIGHT: *Front Cross Version*

I. BACK CROSS VERSION

Rows 1, 3, and 5 (Right side)—K2, (p1, k1) 3 times, p6, k2.
Rows 2, 4, and 6—K8, (p1, k1) 3 times, k2.
Row 7—K2, sl next 7 sts to dpn and hold in back, p5, then (p1, k1) 3 times, p1 (the 7 sts from dpn); k2.
Rows 8, 10, 12, and 14—K3, (p1, k1) 3 times, k7.
Rows 9, 11, and 13—K2, p6, (k1, p1) 3 times, k2.
Row 15—K2, sl next 5 sts to dpn and hold in back, (p1, k1) 3 times, p1—the next 7 sts—then p5 from dpn; k2.
Row 16—Repeat Row 2.

Repeat Rows 1–16.

II. FRONT CROSS VERSION

Rows 1, 3, and 5 (Right side)—K2, p6, (k1, p1) 3 times, k2.
Rows 2, 4, and 6—K3, (p1, k1) 3 times, k7.
Row 7—K2, sl next 5 sts to dpn and hold in front, (p1, k1) 3 times, p1—the next 7 sts—then p5 from dpn; k2.
Rows 8, 10, 12, and 14—K8, (p1, k1) 3 times, k2.
Rows 9, 11, and 13—K2, (p1, k1) 3 times, p6, k2.
Row 15—K2, sl next 7 sts to dpn and hold in front, p5, then (p1, k1) 3 times, p1 (the 7 sts from dpn); k2.
Row 16—Repeat Row 2.

Repeat Rows 1–16.

Wrapped Rib Cable

This is nothing but a simple cable, broken at the sides by an encroachment, at intervals, of the purled background. The result is remarkably pretty and unusual. Recommended for beginners or near-beginners who are looking for an easy but "different" pattern.

Panel of 10 sts.

Rows 1, 3, and 5 (Right side)—P2, k6, p2.
Rows 2, 4, and 6—K2, p6, k2.
Row 7—P2, sl next 3 sts to dpn and hold in back, k3, then k3 from dpn; p2.
Rows 8, 10, and 12—Repeat Row 2.

Rows 9 and 11—Repeat Row 1.
Rows 13, 15, 17, and 19—P4, k2, p4.
Rows 14, 16, 18, and 20—K4, p2, k4.

Repeat Rows 1–20.

Crossed V Stitch

Contributed by Barbara N. Rankin, Cleveland Heights, Ohio

Panel of 15 sts.

NOTES: Front Cross (FC): sl 2 sts to dpn and hold in front, p1, then k2 from dpn.

Back Cross (BC): sl 1 st to dpn and hold in back, k2, then p1 from dpn.

Rows 1 and 3 (Wrong side)—K5, p2, k1, p2, k5.
Row 2—P5, sl next 3 sts to dpn and hold in back, k2, then sl the purl st from dpn back to left-hand needle and purl it, then k2 from dpn; p5.
Row 4—P4, BC, k1, FC, p4.
Row 5 and all subsequent wrong-side rows—Knit all knit sts and purl all purl sts.
Row 6—P3, BC, k1, p1, k1, FC, p3.
Row 8—P2, BC, (k1, p1) twice, k1, FC, p2.
Row 10—P1, BC, (k1, p1) 3 times, k1, FC, p1.
Row 12—BC, (k1, p1) 4 times, k1, FC.
Row 14—K2, p3, k2, p1, k2, p3, k2.

Repeat Rows 1–14.

LEFT: *Wrapped Rib Cable*
CENTER: *Crossed V Stitch*
RIGHT: *Gordian Knot*

Gordian Knot

In spite of its rather forbidding name, this pattern is easy to work. By a clever twist in the cabling technique, the central purl stitches are forced forward to make a tight little knot with the knit ribs crossed behind. The cable appears as a small chain with links tightly tied together.

Panel of 10 sts.

Row 1 (Right side)—(P2, k2) twice, p2.
Row 2—(K2, p2) twice, k2.
Row 3—P2, sl next 4 sts to dpn and hold in front, k2, then sl the 2 purl sts from dpn back to left-hand needle, then pass the dpn with 2 remaining knit sts to back of work; p2 from left-hand needle, then k2 from dpn; p2.
Rows 4, 6, and 8—Repeat Row 2.
Rows 5, 7, and 9—Repeat Row 1.
Row 10—Repeat Row 2.

Repeat Rows 1–10.

Four Cables with Openwork: Picot Eyelet Cable, Waves and Footprints, Highlight Cable, and Brisket Cable

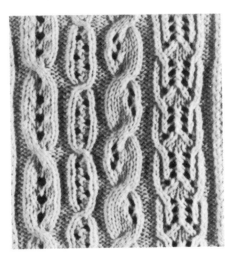

LEFT TO RIGHT:
1. *Picot Eyelet Cable*
2. *Waves and Footprints*
3. *Highlight Cable*
4. *Brisket Cable*

All four of these cables are simple to work, and pretty either single or in combination. They are "idea" patterns, because the knitter can add touches of openwork to other types of cables as well. Only four out of a large number of possibilities are shown here.

I. PICOT EYELET CABLE

Panel of 10 sts.

Row 1 (Wrong side)—K2, p6, k2.
Row 2—P2, k1, k2 tog, (yo) twice, ssk, k1, p2.
Row 3—K2, p2, (k1, p1) into the double yo of previous row, p2, k2.
Row 4—P2, k6, p2.
Row 5—Repeat Row 1.
Row 6—P2, sl next 4 sts to dpn and hold in front, k2, then sl the center 2 sts from dpn back to left-hand needle and knit them, then k2 from dpn; p2.
Rows 7 through 18—Repeat Rows 1 through 4, 3 times more.

Repeat Rows 1–18.

II. WAVES AND FOOTPRINTS

Panel of 8 sts.

Row 1 (Wrong side) and all other wrong-side rows—K2, (p1, k2) twice.
Rows 2, 6, and 10—P2, k1, yo, ssk, k1, p2.
Rows 4 and 8—P2, k1, k2 tog, yo, k1, p2.
Row 12—P2, k4, p2.
Row 14—P2, sl next 3 sts to dpn and hold in back, k1, then sl the center 2 sts from dpn back to left-hand needle and knit them, then k1 from dpn; p2.
Rows 16, 20, and 24—P2, k1, k2 tog, yo, k1, p2.
Rows 18 and 22—P2, k1, yo, ssk, k1, p2.
Row 26—Repeat Row 12.
Row 28—P2, sl next 3 sts to dpn and hold in front, k1, then sl the center 2 sts from dpn back to left-hand needle and knit them, then k1 from dpn; p2.

Repeat Rows 1–28.

III. HIGHLIGHT CABLE

Panel of 10 sts.

Row 1 (Wrong side) and all other wrong-side rows—K2, p6, k2.
Row 2—P2, k6, p2.
Row 4—P2, sl next 3 sts to dpn and hold in back, k3, then k3 from dpn; p2.
Row 6—Repeat Row 2.
Row 8—P2, k1, yo, k2 tog, k3, p2.
Row 10—P2, ssk, yo, k4, p2.
Row 12—Repeat Row 8.
Rows 14, 16, and 18—Repeat Rows 2, 4, and 6.
Row 20—P2, k3, ssk, yo, k1, p2.
Row 22—P2, k4, yo, k2 tog, p2.
Row 24—Repeat Row 20.

Repeat Rows 1–24.

IV. BRISKET CABLE

Panel of 13 sts.

Row 1 (Wrong side) and all other wrong-side rows—K2, p1, k1, p5, k1, p1, k2.
Rows 2, 4, and 6—P2, k1-b, p1, k1-b, yo, sl 1—k2 tog—psso, yo, k1-b, p1, k1-b, p2.
Row 8—P2, sl next 2 sts to dpn and hold in back, k1, then sl the purl st from dpn back to left-hand needle and purl it, then k1 from dpn; k1-b, k1, k1-b, sl next 2 sts to dpn and hold in front, k1, then sl the purl st from dpn back to left-hand needle and purl it, then k1 from dpn; p2.
Row 10—P2, k1-b, p1, yo, ssk, k1, k2 tog, yo, p1, k1-b, p2.

Repeat Rows 1–10.

CENTER PANEL: *Diamond with Chain*
SIDE PANELS: *Bobbled Cable*

Diamond with Chain

NOTES: Front Cross (FC): sl 2 sts to dpn and hold in front, p1, then k2 from dpn.

Back Cross (BC): sl 1 st to dpn and hold in back, k2, then p1 from dpn.

Single Front Cross (SFC): sl 1 st to dpn and hold in front, p1, then k1 from dpn.

Single Back Cross (SBC): sl 1 st to dpn and hold in back, k1, then p1 from dpn.

Single Knit Cross (SKC): Same as SBC, but *knit* both sts.

Row 1 (Wrong side)—K6, p4, k6.
Row 2—P5, BC, FC, p5.
Row 3 and all subsequent wrong-side rows—Knit all knit sts and
  purl all purl sts.
Row 4—P4, BC, k2, FC, p4.
Row 6—P3, BC, p1, SKC, p1, FC, p3.
Row 8—P2, BC, p1, SBC, SFC, p1, FC, p2.
Row 10—P1, BC, p2, (k1, p2) twice, FC, p1.
Row 12—BC, p3, SFC, SBC, p3, FC.
Row 14—K2, p5, SKC, p5, k2.
Row 16—FC, p3, SBC, SFC, p3, BC.
Row 18—P1, FC, p2, (k1, p2) twice, BC, p1.
Row 20—P2, FC, p1, SFC, SBC, p1, BC, p2.
Row 22—P3, FC, p1, SKC, p1, BC, p3.
Row 24—P4, FC, p2, BC, p4.
Row 26—P5, FC, BC, p5.
Row 28—P6, sl next 2 sts to dpn and hold in back, k2, then k2
  from dpn; p6.

Repeat Rows 1–28.

Bobbled Cable

This is a simple eccentric cable with a purled bobble worked
into the broader portion. It is a basic demonstration only; bobbles
may be placed like this on any kind of cable, and in any quantity,
according to the taste of the knitter.

Panel of 11 sts.

Row 1 (Wrong side) and all other wrong-side rows—K2, p7, k2.
Row 2—For a right-twist cable, work Row 2 as follows: P2,
  sl 3 to dpn and hold in back, k4, then k3 from dpn; p2.
    For a left-twist cable, work Row 2 as follows: P2, sl 4 to dpn
    and hold in front, k3, then k4 from dpn; p2.
Row 4—P2, k7, p2.
Rows 6, 10, and 12—Repeat Row 4.
Row 8—Repeat Row 2.
Row 14—P2, k3, Make Bobble in center st as follows: (k1, yo,
  k1, yo, k1) in same st, making 5 sts from one; turn and k5,
  turn and p5, turn and ssk, k1, k2 tog, turn and p3 tog, com-
  pleting bobble; k3, p2.
Row 16—Repeat Row 4.

Repeat Rows 1–16.

2
Cable-Stitch
Patterns

The patterns in this section are distinguished from cables (although they are likewise worked with the aid of a cable needle) because they are intended primarily for use all over a fabric, rather than for use in isolated panels. However, there is nothing to prevent you from using these patterns in panels of one or two repeats if you wish. Use the given multiple of stitches, plus the edge stitches if any. For example, if a cable-stitch pattern is worked on a multiple of 10 stitches plus 5, you could work a single-repeat panel on 15 stitches, or a double-repeat panel on 25 stitches, etc.

Cable-stitch patterns make attractive fabrics, which in most cases have a great deal of depth and dimension to them. Take care, however, with your gauge. These patterns are practically *never* interchangeable with stockinette stitch, because the cabling action pulls the stitches together laterally and gives you quite a few *more* stitches to the inch than you would have in plain knitting. To make a garment wide enough to fit you, it is necessary to cast on more than your "standard" number of stitches. Therefore it is important to make test swatches and check the number of stitches—or pattern repeats, if you prefer to figure it that way—in any desired width measurement. Length measurements, however, will remain approximately average; the row gauge changes very little, if at all.

Cable-stitch patterns are frequently worked in medium to heavy yarn, to make firm, thick fabrics for sweaters, jackets, afghans, and coats. But they can be worked in fine yarn, too. There is no reason why a dress or baby sweater, in thin fingering yarn, cannot be worked in a cable-stitch pattern. Remember to use a cable needle *thinner* than the needles being used for the rest of the knitting, so the stitches will not be over-stretched in cabling (this is always a good idea for any kind of cabled pattern).

These patterns can be combined, too. One pattern might be used as a central panel, another for the remainder of the garment. Or perhaps you would like to make a set of "matching" cushions, each one in a different cable-stitch pattern. The possibilities, as usual, are endless.

Barrel Stitch

Barrel Stitch

Contributed by Dorothy M. Singer, Concord, Vermont

This pattern comes from France, and makes a fabric that is pretty on both sides. It can be either a close fabric or one that is quite "open", depending on the weight of the yarn used and the degree to which it is stretched.

Multiple of 10 sts plus 8.

Rows 1, 3, and 5 (Wrong side)—K1, * k6, p4; rep from *, end k7.

Row 2—K1, * p6, sl next 2 sts to dpn and hold in back, k2, then k2 from dpn; rep from *, end p6, k1.

Row 4—K1, * p6, yo, k2 tog-b, k2 tog, yo; rep from *, end p6, k1.

Row 6—Repeat Row 2.

Row 7—K1, * k3 tog-b, k3 tog, pass the first of these 2 sts over the second; p4; rep from *, end last repeat k1 instead of p4.

Row 8—K1, * (k1, p1) 3 times in the next st, making 6 sts from one; yo, k2 tog-b, k2 tog, yo; rep from *, end (k1, p1) 3 times in next st, k1.

Repeat Rows 1–8.

Wave of Honey Stitch

Wave of Honey Stitch

A single-stitch version of the Aran Honeycomb which makes a beautiful three-dimensional lattice pattern when used over a large number of stitches. It is somewhat tedious to work, due to the necessity of using the cable needle for every stitch on every right-side row. But if you are handy with the cable needle, the results of this pattern are well worth the trouble.

Multiple of 4 sts.

Rows 1 and 3 (Wrong side)—Purl.

Row 2—* Sl 1 to dpn and hold in back, k1, k the st from dpn; sl next st to dpn and hold in front, k1, k the st from dpn; rep from * across.

Row 4—* Sl 1 to dpn and hold in front, k1, k the st from dpn; sl next st to dpn and hold in back, k1, k the st from dpn; rep from * across.

Repeat Rows 1–4.

Aran Honeycomb

The Aran Honeycomb is a number of Chain Cables repeated across the fabric, which gives a three-dimensional effect. It is frequently used in fisherman sweaters.

Multiple of 8 sts.

Row 1 (Wrong side) and all other wrong-side rows—Purl.
Row 2—* Sl 2 to dpn and hold in back, k2, k2 from dpn; sl 2 to dpn and hold in front, k2, k2 from dpn; rep from * across.
Row 4—Knit.
Row 6—* Sl 2 to dpn and hold in front, k2, k2 from dpn; sl 2 to dpn and hold in back, k2, k2 from dpn; rep from * across.
Row 8—Knit.

Repeat Rows 1–8.

VARIATION: *ELONGATED ARAN HONEYCOMB*

If desired, the Honeycomb can be elongated by inserting two extra plain rows between cabling rows. This gives the "honey-cells" a rather square shape.

Multiple of 8 sts.

Row 1 (Wrong side) and all other wrong-side rows—Purl.
Row 2—As Row 2, above.
Rows 4 and 6—Knit.
Row 8—As Row 6, above.
Rows 10 and 12—Knit.

Repeat Rows 1–12.

ABOVE: *Aran Honeycomb*
BELOW: *Elongated Aran Honeycomb*

Shadow Cable

This is an allover pattern related to Basket Cable, except that the cabled stitches are staggered and do not cross one another.

Multiple of 8 sts plus 2.

Row 1 (Wrong side) and all other wrong-side rows—Purl.
Row 2—Knit.
Row 4—K1, * sl next 2 sts to dpn and hold in back, k2, k2 from dpn, k4; rep from *, end k1.
Row 6—Knit.
Row 8—K1, * k4, sl next 2 sts to dpn and hold in front, k2, k2 from dpn; rep from *, end k1.

Repeat Rows 1–8.

Shadow Cable

Basket Cable

Basket Cable

This pattern is exceedingly dense in the lateral dimension, as might be expected when 4 stitches are cabled over 4 stitches all the way across the row. Basket Cable is popularly used in panel form for fancy cable sweaters, though in fact the Close-Woven Basket Lattice gives much the same effect with a much neater appearance. When Basket Cable is used as a panel, the 4 edge stitches may be omitted or converted into purl stitches.

Multiple of 8 sts plus 4.

Rows 1, 3, and 5 (Wrong side)—K2, purl to last 2 sts, k2.
Rows 2 and 4—Knit.
Row 6—K2, * sl next 4 sts to dpn and hold in back, k4, then k4 from dpn; rep from *, end k2.
Rows 7, 9, and 11—K2, purl to last 2 sts, k2.
Rows 8 and 10—Knit.
Row 12—K6, * sl next 4 sts to dpn and hold in front, k4, then k4 from dpn; rep from *, end k6.

Repeat Rows 1–12.

Clustered Cable or Cable Check

Clustered Cable or Cable Check

This is a simple German pattern consisting of knit-purl checks, with a single cable cross worked into each knit check.

Multiple of 12 sts plus 6.

Rows 1 and 3 (Right side)—P6, * k6, p6; rep from * across.
Rows 2 and 4—K6, * p6, k6; rep from * across.
Row 5—P6, * sl next 3 to dpn and hold in back, k3, k3 from dpn, p6; rep from *.
Row 6—K6, * p6, k6; rep from * across.
Row 7—P6, * k6, p6; rep from * across.
Row 8—K6, * p6, k6; rep from * across.
Rows 9 and 11—K6, * p6, k6; rep from * across.
Rows 10 and 12—P6, * k6, p6; rep from * across.
Row 13—* Sl 3 to dpn and hold in back, k3, k3 from dpn, p6; rep from *, end sl 3 to dpn and hold in back, k3, k3 from dpn.
Row 14—P6, * k6, p6; rep from * across.
Row 15—K6, * p6, k6; rep from * across.
Row 16—P6, * k6, p6; rep from * across.

Repeat Rows 1–16.

Lace Cable or Germaine Stitch

This pattern is ideal for the knitter who wants to use a dainty openwork but likes to work a few cables into everything. The lace portion of the pattern is recognizable as Little Arrowhead. The same combination comes out equally well with the larger-patterned Arrowhead Lace: simple cables worked in between the lace panels.

Multiple of 11 sts plus 7.

Row 1 (Wrong side) and all other wrong-side rows—Purl.

Row 2—K1, * yo, ssk, k1, k2 tog, yo, k6; rep from * to last 6 sts, end yo, ssk, k1, k2 tog, yo, k1.

Row 4—K2, * yo, sl 1—k2 tog—psso, yo, k1, sl next 3 sts to dpn and hold in back, k3, then k3 from dpn, k1; rep from * to last 5 sts, end yo, sl 1—k2 tog—psso, yo, k2.

Row 6—Repeat Row 2.

Row 8—K2, * yo, sl 1—k2 tog—psso, yo, k8; rep from * to last 5 sts, end yo, sl 1—k2 tog—psso, yo, k2.

Repeat Rows 1–8.

Lace Cable or Germaine Stitch

Diagonal Wave

This pattern has one feature that is unique among cable patterns—it looks the same on both sides. As given, the waves run upward to the right. It is a simple matter to reverse the diagonals, making the waves run to the left, by slipping 3 knit sts to the cable needle, holding them in front, and purling 3 sts behind.

Multiple of 6 sts plus 3.

Rows 1, 3, and 5   (Wrong side)—K3, * p3, k3; rep from *.

Rows 2 and 4—P3, * k3, p3; rep from *.

Row 6—* Sl 3 sts to dpn and hold in back, k3, then p3 from dpn; rep from *, end k3.

Rows 7, 9, and 11—P3, * k3, p3; rep from *.

Rows 8 and 10—K3, * p3, k3; rep from *.

Row 12—P3, * sl next 3 sts to dpn and hold in back, k3, then p3 from dpn; rep from *.

Repeat Rows 1–12.

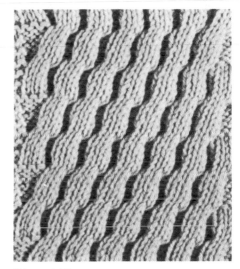

Diagonal Wave

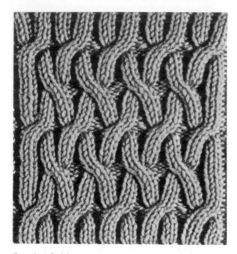

Lattice Cable

Lattice Cable

An allover pattern of knit stitches woven across a purl-stitch ground.

Multiple of 8 sts plus 2.

Rows 1, 3, 5 and 7 (Wrong side)—K2, * p2, k2; rep from *.
Rows 2, 4, and 6—P2, * k2, p2; rep from *.
Row 8—P2, * sl next 4 to dpn and hold in back, k2, sl the 2 p sts from dpn back to left-hand needle and p them; k2 from dpn, p2; rep from *.
Rows 9–15—Repeat Rows 1–7.
Row 16—P2, k2, * p2, sl the next 4 sts to dpn and hold in front, k2, sl the 2 p sts from dpn back to left-hand needle and p them; k2 from dpn; rep from *, end p2, k2, p2.

Repeat Rows 1–16.

Basic Lattice

Basic Lattice

The cabled lattice is referred to as "basic" because so many other cable-stitch patterns are developed from it. The principle is simply that knit stitches are "traveled" diagonally across a ground of purl stitches, using the cable needle to move them along.

Note that in this pattern the Back Knit Cross and Front Knit Cross may be omitted from Rows 1 and 9, instead working these rows in straight knit and purl stitches as Row 2. In this case the lattice does not cross or "weave", but forms alternating waves which create a pattern known as Hourglass.

Another pleasing variation is made when all knit stitches on the right side are knitted through the back loops, thus being crossed.

Multiple of 8 sts.

NOTES: Back Cross (BC)—Sl 1 st to dpn and hold in back, k1, then p the st from dpn.

Front Cross (FC)—sl 1 st to dpn and hold in front, p1, then k the st from dpn.

Back Knit Cross (BKC)—sl 1 st to dpn and hold in back, k1, then k the st from dpn.

Front Knit Cross (FKC)—sl 1 st to dpn and hold in front, k1, then k the st from dpn.

Row 1 (Right side)—P3, BKC, * p6, BKC; rep from *, end p3.
Row 2 and all other wrong-side rows—Knit all knit sts and purl all purl sts.
Row 3—P2, * BC, FC, p4; rep from *, end BC, FC, p2.
Row 5—P1, * BC, p2, FC, p2; rep from *, end BC, p2, FC, p1.

Row 7—* BC, p4, FC; rep from *.

Row 9—K1, * p6, FKC; rep from *, end p6, k1.

Row 11—* FC, p4, BC; rep from *.

Row 13—P1, * FC, p2, BC, p2, rep from *, end FC, p2, BC, p1.

Row 15—P2, * FC, BC, p4; rep from *, end FC, BC, p2.

Row 16—See Row 2.

Repeat Rows 1–16.

Ribbed Lattice With Bobbles

Bobbles made by this method are nubby and stiff, rather than loose and "bobbly". This is a decided advantage if the knitted article is to withstand hard use. Note that Row 1 is a preparation row, omitted from subsequent repeats.

Multiple of 20 sts plus 2.

NOTES: Back Cross (BC): sl 1 st to dpn and hold in back, k1-b, then p1 from dpn. Front Cross (FC): sl 1 st to dpn and hold in front, p1, then k1-b from dpn.

Row 1 (Right side–preparation)—P6, * (k1-b, p1) twice, k2-b, (p1, k1-b) twice, p10; rep from *, end last repeat p6.

Row 2—K6, * (p1-b, k1) twice, p2-b, (k1, p1-b) twice, k10; rep from *, end last repeat k6.

Row 3—P6, * k1-b, p1, k1-b, on next 4 sts Make Bobble (MB) as follows: (k4, turn, p4, turn) 3 times, then pick up a loop from the first row of bobble and knit it tog with 1st st on left-hand needle; k2, then pick up a loop from 1st row of bobble and knit it tog with next st, completing bobble; k1-b, p1, k1-b, p10; rep from *, end last repeat p6.

Row 4—K6, * (p1-b, k1) twice, p2-b, (k1, p1-b) twice, k10; rep from *, end last repeat k6.

Row 5—P5, * (BC) 3 times, (FC) 3 times, p8; rep from *, end last repeat p5.

Row 6 and all subsequent wrong-side rows: Knit all knit sts and p-b all purl sts.

Row 7—P4, * (BC) 3 times, p2, (FC) 3 times, p6; rep from *, end last repeat p4.

Row 9—P3, * (BC) 3 times, p4, (FC) 3 times, p4; rep from *, end last repeat p3.

Row 11—P2, * (BC) 3 times, p6, (FC) 3 times, p2; rep from *.

Row 13—P1, * (BC) 3 times, p8, (FC) 3 times; rep from *, end p1.

Row 15—P1, MB on next 4 sts, k1-b, * p10, k1-b, p1, k1-b, MB on next 4 sts, k1-b, p1, k1-b; rep from *, end p10, k1-b, MB on next 4 sts, p1.

Row 16 (Wrong side)—K1, * (p1-b, k1) twice, p1-b, k10, (p1-b, k1) twice, p1-b; rep from *, end k1.

Row 17—P1, * (FC) 3 times, p8, (BC) 3 times; rep from *, end p1.

Row 19—P2, * (FC) 3 times, p6, (BC) 3 times, p2; rep from *.

Row 21—P3, * (FC) 3 times, p4, (BC) 3 times, p4; rep from *, end last repeat p3.

Row 23—P4, * (FC) 3 times, p2, (BC) 3 times, p6; rep from *, end last repeat p4.

Row 25—P5, * (FC) 3 times, (BC) 3 times, p8; rep from *, end last repeat p5.

Omitting Row 1, repeat Rows 2–25.

Ribbed Lattice with Bobbles

Close-Woven Basket Lattice

Close-Woven Basket Lattice

This pattern gives a dense texture in which the illusion of diagonal basketweaving is extremely realistic.

Multiple of 6 sts plus 2.

Row 1 (Wrong side)—K2, * p4, k2; rep from *.

Row 2—P2, * sl 2 sts to dpn and hold in back, k2, then k2 from dpn; p2; rep from *.

Row 3 and all other wrong-side rows—Knit the knit sts and purl the purl sts.

Row 4—P1, * sl 1 st to dpn and hold in back, k2, then p the st from dpn (Back Cross or BC); sl next 2 sts to dpn and hold in front, p1, then k2 from dpn (Front Cross or FC); rep from *, end p1.

Row 6—P1, k2, p2, * sl next 2 sts to dpn and hold in front, k2, then k2 from dpn; p2; rep from *, end k2, p1.

Row 8—P1, * FC, BC; rep from *, end p1.

Repeat Rows 1–8.

Interlocking Lattice

Interlocking Lattice

In this fascinating pattern the sides of the lattice diamonds are twisted around one another. (See Basic Lattice).

Multiple of 6 sts plus 2.

NOTES: For Back Cross, Front Cross, Back Knit Cross and Front Knit Cross, see Notes to Basic Lattice.

Row 1 (Wrong side)—K1, p1, * k4, p2; rep from *, end k4, p1, k1.

Row 2—P1, * FC, p2, BC; rep from *, end p1.

Row 3 and all other wrong-side rows—Knit all knit sts and purl all purl sts.

Row 4—P2, * FC, BC, p2; rep from *.

Row 6—P3, * BKC, p4; rep from *, end last rep p3.

Row 8—P2, * BC, FC, p2; rep from *.

Row 10—P2, * FC, BC, p2; rep from *.

Row 12—As Row 6.

Row 14—P2, * BC, FC, p2; rep from *.

Row 16—P1, * BC, p2, FC; rep from *, end p1.

Row 18—BC, p4, * FKC, p4; rep from *, end FC.

Row 20—K1, p4, * BC, FC, p2; rep from *, end p2, k1.

Row 22—K1, p4, * FC, BC, p2; rep from *, end p2, k1.

Row 24—FC, p4, * FKC, p4; rep from *, end BC.

Repeat Rows 1–24.

Double Hourglass

This is a very handsome pattern of the lattice type, excellent for sweaters. It can be enriched with bobbles or embroidery—a "lazy-daisy", a "snowflake", or some small cross-stitch motif in the center of each diamond of purl. For further embellishment, the knit stitches can be either Crossed or Twisted.

For a single "Hourglass", see Basic Lattice.

Double Hourglass

Multiple of 14 sts plus 2.

NOTES: Back Cross (BC)—sl 1 st to dpn and hold in back, k1, then p1 from dpn. Front Cross (FC)—sl 1 st to dpn and hold in front, p1, then k1 from dpn.

Row 1 (Wrong side)—K1, * p1, k2, p1, k6, p1, k2, p1; rep from *, end k1.
Row 2—P1, * FC, p1, FC, p4, BC, p1, BC; rep from *, end p1.
Row 3 and all other wrong-side rows—Knit all knit sts and purl all purl sts.
Row 4—P1, * (p1, FC) twice, p2, (BC, p1) twice; rep from *, end p1.
Row 6—P1, * p2, FC, p1, FC, BC, p1, BC, p2; rep from *, end p1.
Row 8—Knit all knit sts and purl all purl sts.
Row 10—P1, * p2, BC, p1, BC, FC, p1, FC, p2; rep from *, end p1.
Row 12—P1, * (p1, BC) twice, p2, (FC, p1) twice; rep from *, end p1.
Row 14—P1, * BC, p1, BC, p4, FC, p1, FC; rep from *, end p1.
Row 16—Knit all knit sts and purl all purl sts.

Repeat Rows 1–16.

Fancy Moss Stitch Lattice

This pattern has an unusual three-stitch cross from the wrong side in Rows 1 and 9, which imparts a slightly spiral pull to the diagonal ribs of the lattice. If desired, the reverse cross can be omitted from Rows 1 and 9, instead working these three stitches simply "p1, k1, p1". The resulting pattern will be a most attractive Moss Stitch Hourglass.

Fancy Moss Stitch Lattice

Multiple of 14 sts plus 13.

NOTES: Front Cross (FC): Sl 2 sts to dpn and hold in front, p1, then k2 from dpn. Back Cross (BC): Sl 1 st to dpn and hold in back, k2, then p1 from dpn. Reverse Front Cross (RFC; worked from wrong side): Sl 2 sts to dpn and hold in front, p1, then sl the knit st from dpn back to left-hand needle and knit it, then p1 from dpn. Reverse Back Cross (RBC; worked from wrong side): Sl 2 sts to dpn and hold in back, p1, then sl the knit st from dpn back to left-hand needle and knit it, then p1 from dpn.

Row 1 (Wrong side)—P2, * (k1, p1) 5 times, RBC, p1; rep from *, end (k1, p1) 4 times, k1, p2.

Row 2—FC, (p1, k1) 3 times, p1, BC, * k1, FC, (p1, k1) 3 times, p1, BC; rep from *.

Rows 3, 5, and 7—Knit all knit sts and purl all purl sts.

Row 4—K1, FC, (p1, k1) twice, p1, BC, k1, * p1, k1, FC, (p1, k1) twice, p1, BC, k1; rep from *.

Row 6—P1, k1, FC, p1, k1, p1, BC, k1, p1, * k1, p1, k1, FC, p1, k1, p1, BC, k1, p1; rep from *.

Row 8—K1, p1, k1, FC, p1, BC, k1, p1, k1, * (p1, k1) twice, FC, p1, BC, k1, p1, k1; rep from *.

Row 9—(P1, k1) twice, * p1, RFC, (p1, k1) 5 times; rep from *, end p1, RFC, p1, (k1, p1) twice.

Row 10—P1, k1, p1, BC, k1, FC, p1, k1, p1, * (k1, p1) twice, BC, k1, FC, p1, k1, p1; rep from *.

Rows 11, 13, and 15—Knit all knit sts and purl all purl sts.

Row 12—K1, p1, BC, k1, p1, k1, FC, p1, k1, * p1, k1, p1, BC, k1, p1, k1, FC, p1, k1; rep from *.

Row 14—P1, BC, (k1, p1) twice, k1, FC, p1, * k1, p1, BC, (k1, p1) twice, k1, FC, p1, k1; rep from *.

Row 16—BC, (k1, p1) 3 times, k1, FC, * p1, BC, (k1, p1) 3 times, k1, FC; rep from *.

Repeat Rows 1–16.

LEFT: *Traveling Cable, left*
RIGHT: *Traveling Cable, right*

Traveling Cable

In this pattern the cables can be moved either to the right or to the left. Either version is pretty as an allover pattern, but if there are two panels of Traveling Cable, one on each side of a common center, then one of each version should be used.

TRAVELING CABLE, LEFT

Multiple of 5 sts plus 1.

Rows 1 and 3 (Right side)—P1, * k4, p1; rep from *.

Rows 2, 4, and 6—K1, * p4, k1; rep from *.

Row 5—P1, * sl next 2 sts to dpn and hold in front, k2, then k2 from dpn (Front Cross, FC), p1; rep from *.

Rows 7 and 9—K1, * p1, k4; rep from *.

Rows 8, 10, and 12—* P4, k1; rep from *, end p1.

Row 11—K1, * p1, FC; rep from *.

Rows 13 and 15—K2, * p1, k4; rep from *, end p1, k3.

Rows 14, 16, and 18—P3, * k1, p4; rep from *, end k1, p2.

Rows 17—K2, * p1, FC; rep from *, end p1, k3.

Rows 19 and 21—K3, * p1, k4; rep from *, end p1, k2.
Rows 20, 22, and 24—P2, * k1, p4; rep from *, end k1, p3.
Row 23—K3, * p1, FC; rep from *, end p1, k2.
Rows 25 and 27—* K4, p1; rep from *, end k1.
Rows 26 and 28—P1, * k1, p4; rep from *.
Row 29—* FC, p1; rep from *, end k1.
Row 30—P1, * k1, p4; rep from *.

Repeat Rows 1-30.

TRAVELING CABLE, RIGHT

Multiple of 5 sts plus 1.

Rows 1 and 3 (Right side)—P1, * k4, p1; rep from *.
Rows 2, 4, and 6—K1, * p4, k1; rep from *.
Row 5—P1, * sl next 2 sts to dpn and hold in back, k2; then
   k2 from dpn (Back Cross, BC), p1; rep from *.
Rows 7 and 9—* K4, p1; rep from *, end k1.
Rows 8, 10, and 12—P1, * k1, p4; rep from *.
Row 11—* BC, p1; rep from *, end k1.
Rows 13 and 15—K3, * p1, k4; rep from *, end p1, k2.
Rows 14, 16, and 18—P2, * k1, p4; rep from *, end k1, p3.
Row 17—K3, * p1, BC; rep from *, end p1, k2.
Rows 19 and 21—K2, * p1, k4; rep from *, end p1, k3.
Rows 20, 22, and 24—P3, * k1, p4; rep from *, end k1, p2.
Row 23—K2, * p1, BC; rep from *, end p1, k3.
Rows 25 and 27—K1, * p1, k4; rep from *.
Rows 26 and 28—* P4, k1; rep from *, end p1.
Row 29—K1, * p1, BC; rep from *.
Row 30—* P4, k1; rep from *, end p1.

Repeat Rows 1-30.

Traveling Rib Pattern

Multiple of 6 sts plus 4.

Rows 1 and 3 (Wrong side)—P1, * k2, p1; rep from *.
Row 2—K1, * p2, k1; rep from *.
Row 4—* Sl 3 sts to dpn and hold in back, k1, then holding
   yarn in front, sl the 2 purl sts from dpn back to left-hand
   needle and purl them; then knit remaining st from dpn
   (Cross 4); p2; rep from *, end Cross 4.
Rows 5, 6, and 7—Repeat Rows 1, 2, and 3.
Row 8—K1, p2, * Cross 4, p2; rep from *, end k1.

Repeat Rows 1-8.

Traveling Rib Pattern

83

Bell Rib Pattern

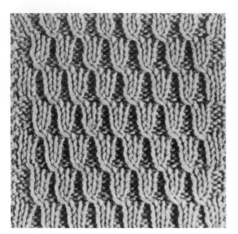

Bell Rib Pattern

This pattern tends to draw together quite strongly when being worked, and in blocking it must be well stretched laterally. The texture is quite pretty. After it is stretched, the little indented "bells" in purl stitches can be seen.

Multiple of 4 sts plus 2.

Rows 1, 3, and 5 (Wrong side)—P2, * k2, p2; rep from *.

Rows 2 and 4—K2, * p2, k2; rep from *.

Row 6—K1, * sl next st to dpn and hold in front, p1, skip 1 st and knit the next st inserting the point of needle into the st and then around the right-hand side of skipped st to catch yarn, then complete the knitting of this st drawing it *over* the skipped st and off needle; yarn to front and knit the st from dpn; then p1 (the skipped st); rep from *, end k1.

Rows 7, 9, and 11—K2, * p2, k2; rep from *.

Rows 8 and 10—P2, * k2, p2; rep from *.

Row 12—K1, skip next st and knit the 2nd st drawing it over skipped st as before; purl the skipped st, * repeat from * of Row 6, end sl 1 to dpn and hold in front, p1, k1 from dpn, k1.

Repeat Rows 1–12.

Diamond Window Pattern

Diamond Window Pattern

Most cable patterns are composed of motifs in knit stitches, displayed against a purled background. This pattern is the reverse: the diamond motifs are purled (and therefore indented) while the borders and background are made of knit stitches. If desired, the pattern can be worked the other way, with knit diamonds on a purled ground, simply by reading "knit" for "purl" and vice versa.

This is a very handsome pattern for a sweater, and readily lends itself to further embellishment with touches of embroidery or bobbles or some other accent worked into the center of each diamond.

Multiple of 26 sts.

NOTES: Back Knit Cross (BKC): sl 1 st to dpn and hold in back, k2, then k1 from dpn. Front Knit Cross (FKC): sl 2 sts to dpn and hold in front, k1, then k2 from dpn. Back Purl Cross

(BPC): sl 1 st to dpn and hold in back, k2, then p1 from dpn.
Front Purl Cross (FPC): sl 2 sts to dpn and hold in front, p1,
then k2 from dpn.

Row 1 (Wrong side)—* K5, p16, k5; rep from *.
Row 2—* P4, BKC, k12, FKC, p4; rep from *.
Row 3 and all subsequent wrong-side rows—Knit all knit sts and purl all purl sts.
Row 4—* P3, BKC, k4, BPC, FPC, k4, FKC, p3; rep from *
Row 6—* P2, BKC, k4, BPC, p2, FPC, k4, FKC, p2; rep from *.
Row 8—* P1, BKC, k4, BPC, p4, FPC, k4, FKC, p1; rep from *.
Row 10—* BKC, k4, BPC, p6, FPC, k4, FKC; rep from *.
Row 12—* K6, BPC, p8, FPC, k6; rep from *.
Row 14—* K6, FKC, p8, BKC, k6; rep from *.
Row 16—* FPC, k4, FKC, p6, BKC, k4, BPC; rep from *.
Row 18—* P1, FPC, k4, FKC, p4, BKC, k4, BPC, p1; rep from *.
Row 20—* P2, FPC, k4, FKC, p2, BKC, k4, BPC, p2; rep from *.
Row 22—* P3, FPC, k4, FKC, BKC, k4, BPC, p3; rep from *.
Row 24—* P4, FPC, k12, BPC, p4; rep from *.

Repeat Rows 1–24.

Little Bow Twist

This is a charming spot-pattern on a purled fabric.

Multiple of 12 sts plus 7.

Row 1 (Wrong side)—Knit.
Rows 2, 4, 8, and 12—P1, * k1, p3, k1, p7; rep from *, end k1,
p3, k1, p1.
Rows 3, 5, 7, 9, 11, and 13—K1, * p1, k3, p1, k7; rep from *,
end p1, k3, p1, k1.
Rows 6 and 10—P1, * sl next 4 sts to dpn and hold in back, k1,
then sl the 3 purl sts back to left-hand needle and purl them;
then knit the last st from dpn; p7; rep from *, end last
repeat p1.
Row 14—Purl.
Row 15—Knit.
Rows 16, 18, 22, and 26—P7, * k1, p3, k1, p7; rep from *.
Rows 17, 19, 21, 23, 25, and 27—K7, * p1, k3, p1, k7; rep
from *.
Rows 20 and 24—P7, * sl next 4 sts to dpn and hold in back,
k1, then sl the 3 purl sts back to left-hand needle and purl
them; then knit the last st from dpn; p7, rep from *.
Row 28—Purl.

Repeat Rows 1–28.

Little Bow Twist

Arrow Cable

Arrow Cable

This is a nice pattern for either vertical or horizontal panels.

Multiple of 16 sts plus 4.

NOTES: Front Cross (FC): sl 1 st to dpn and hold in front, p1, then k1 from dpn. Back Cross (BC): sl 1 st to dpn and hold in back, k1, then p1 from dpn. Cable 4: sl 2 sts to dpn and hold in back, k2, then k2 from dpn.

Row 1 (Wrong side)—P4, * p1, k3, p4, k3, p5; rep from *.
Row 2—K4, * FC, p2, k4, p2, BC, k4; rep from *.
Rows 3, 5, and 7—Knit all knit sts and purl all purl sts.
Row 4—Cable 4, * p1, FC, p1, Cable 4, p1, BC, p1, Cable 4; rep from *.
Row 6—K4, * p2, FC, k4, BC, p2, k4; rep from *.
Row 8—Cable 4, * p4, Cable 4; rep from *.

Repeat Rows 1–8.

Acorn Pattern

Acorn Pattern

This is an old English pattern that makes a handsome novelty fabric.

Multiple of 10 sts plus 2.

Row 1 (Right side-preparation row)—K1, p3, k4, * p6, k4; rep from *, end p3, k1.
Row 2—K4, p4, * k6, p4; rep from *, end k4.
Row 3—K1, p1, * sl next 2 sts to dpn and hold in back, k2, then p2 from dpn (Back Cross, BC); insert needle under running thread between st just worked and the next st, and (k1, p1) into this thread; sl next 2 sts to dpn and hold in front, p2, then k2 from dpn (Front Cross, FC); p2; rep from * to last 2 sts, end last repeat p1, k1.
Rows 4 and 6—K2, * p2, k2; rep from *.
Row 5—K1, p1, * k2, p2; rep from *, end k2, p1, k1.
Row 7—K2, * ssk, p6, k2 tog, k2; rep from *.
Row 8—K1, p2, k6, * p4, k6; rep from *, end p2, k1.
Row 9—K1, insert needle under running thread and knit once into this thread, * FC, p2, BC, (k1, p1) into running thread; rep from *, end FC, p2, BC, knit once into running thread, k1.
Rows 10 and 12—K1, p1, * k2, p2; rep from *, end k2, p1, k1.
Row 11—K2, * p2, k2; rep from *.
Row 13—K1, p3, * k2 tog, k2, ssk, p6; rep from *, end k2 tog, k2, ssk, p3, k1.

Omit Row 1, Repeat Rows 2–13.

Cathedral Pattern

This marvelous pattern has a little of everything—lace, cabling, and bobbles. It is classified under Cable Patterns because it does require the use of the cable needle, and the lace part of the pattern is more like a series of accents in an otherwise solid fabric.

The Cathedral is one of those ever-fascinating pictures in yarn. Its realism is astonishing. The beautiful "stained-glass windows" are built up of Vertical Lace Trellis—an indication of how imagination and a general knowledge of simple pattern stitches can be used to make almost any sort of artistic effect.

Cathedral Pattern

Panel of 25 sts.

Row 1 (Right side)—P2, k4, (yo, k2 tog) 7 times, k3, p2.

Row 2—K2, p21, k2.

Row 3—P2, k3, (ssk, yo) 7 times, k4, p2.

Row 4 K2, p21, k2.

Rows 5 through 20—Repeat Rows 1–4 four times more.

Row 21—P2, k4, (yo, ssk) twice, yo, sl 2 knitwise—k1—p2sso, yo, (k2 tog, yo) 3 times, k4, p2.

Row 22—K2, p21, k2.

Row 23 P2, sl next 2 sts to dpn and hold in front, p1, then k2 from dpn (Front Cross or FC); k2, (yo, ssk) twice, yo, sl 2 knitwise—k1—p2sso, yo, (k2 tog, yo) twice, k2, sl next st to dpn and hold in back, k2, then p1 from dpn (Back Cross or BC); p2.

Row 24—K3, p19, k3.

Row 25—P3, FC, k2, yo, ssk, yo, sl 2 knitwise—k1—p2sso, yo, (k2 tog, yo) twice, k2, BC, p3.

Row 26—K4, p17, k4

Row 27—P4, FC, k2, yo, ssk, yo, sl 2 knitwise—k1—p2sso, yo, k2 tog, yo, k2, BC, p5.

Row 28—K5, p15, k5.

Row 29—P5, FC, k2, yo, sl 2 knitwise—k1—p2sso, yo, k2 tog, yo, k2, BC, p4.

Row 30—K6, p13, k6.

Row 31—P6, FC, k2, yo, sl 2 knitwise—k1—p2sso, yo, k2, BC, p6.

Row 32—K7, p11, k7.

Row 33—P7, FC, k1, k2 tog, yo, k2, BC, p7.

Row 34—K8, p9, k8.

Row 35—P8, FC, k3, BC, p8.

Row 36—K9, p7, k9.

Row 37—P9, FC, k1, BC, p9.

Row 38—K10, p5, k10.

Row 39—P11, k1, make Bobble in center st as follows: (k1, yo, k1, yo, k1) in same st; turn and p5; turn and k5; turn and p1, p3 tog, p1; turn and sl 2 knitwise—k1—p2sso; Bobble completed; k1, p11.

Row 40—K12, p1-b, k12.

Row 41—Purl.

Row 42—Knit.

Repeat Rows 1–42.

Flying Wings Pattern

Flying Wings Pattern

It does not put too heavy a burden on the imagination to see in this pattern a flock of birds in flight. It is an ingenious combination of twist and cable stitches, making a closely woven texture that is attractive either in panels of 3 or 4 repeats or as an allover fabric.

Multiple of 6 sts.

Row 1 (Right side)—Knit.

Row 2—Purl.

Row 3—* Skip 2 sts, knit into 3rd st on left-hand needle and pull through a loop; then knit 1st and 2nd sts and sl all 3 sts from needle together; sl next st to dpn and hold in front, k2, then k1 from dpn; rep from *.

Row 4—P5, * skip 1 st and purl the 2nd st on left-hand needle, then purl the skipped st and sl both sts from needle together; p4; rep from *, end p1.

Repeat Rows 1–4.

Serpentine Cables

Serpentine Cables

When repeated over a large number of stitches, this pattern gives a truly wonderful array of interlinked cables which appear more complicated than they are.

Multiple of 8 sts plus 4. (A minimum of 20 sts is required to show pattern.)

NOTES: Front Cross or FC—sl 2 k sts to dpn, hold in front, p1, then k2 from dpn. Back Cross or BC—sl 1 p st to dpn, hold in back, k2, then p1 from dpn. Front Double Knit Cross or FDKC—sl 2 k sts to dpn, hold in front, k2, then k2 from dpn. Back Double Knit Cross or BDKC—sl 2 k sts to dpn, hold in back, k2, then k2 from dpn.

Row 1 (Wrong side)—K2, p2, * k4, p4; rep from *, end k4, p2, k2.

Row 2—P2, * FC, p2, BC; rep from *, end p2.

Row 3 and all other wrong-side rows—Knit all knit sts and purl all purl sts.

Row 4—P3, * FC, BC, p2; rep from *, end p1.

Row 6—* P4, BDKC; rep from *, end p4.

Row 8—P3, * BC, FC, p2; rep from *, end p1.

Row 10—Knit all knit sts and purl all purl sts.

Row 12—P3, * FC, BC, p2; rep from *, end p1.

Row 14—* P4, BDKC; rep from *, end p4.
Row 16—P3, * BC, FC, p2; rep from *, end p1.
Row 18—P2, * BC, p2, FC; rep from *, end p2.
Row 20—P1, BC, * p4, FDKC; rep from *, end p4, FC, p1.
Row 22—BC, p4, * BC, FC, p2; rep from *, end p2, FC.
Row 24—Knit all knit sts and purl all purl sts.
Row 26—FC, p4, * FC, BC, p2; rep from *, end p2, BC.
Row 28—P1, FC, * p4, FDKC; rep from *, end p4, BC, p1.

Repeat Rows 1–28.

Plaid Lattice

This is a double pattern; a lattice of two-stitch ribs is superimposed upon another lattice of one-stitch ribs. One single panel, 16 sts wide, makes the popular "X-in-a-diamond" cable.

Plaid Lattice

Multiple of 14 sts plus 2.

Row 1 (Wrong side)—K1, * p1, k4, p4, k4, p1; rep from *, end k1.
Row 2—P1, k1-b, * p4, sl 2 sts to dpn and hold in front, k2, then k2 from dpn; p4, sl 1 st to dpn and hold in front, k1-b, then k1-b from dpn; rep from * to last 2 sts, end last repeat k1-b, p1.
Row 3 and all other wrong-side rows—Knit all knit sts and purl all purl sts.
Row 4—P1, * sl 1 st to dpn and hold in front, p1, then k1-b from dpn (Single Front Cross, SFC); p2; sl 1 st to dpn and hold in back, k2, then p1 from dpn (Back Cross, BC); sl 2 sts to dpn and hold in front, p1, then k2 from dpn (Front Cross, FC); p2; sl 1 st to dpn and hold in back, k1-b, then p1 from dpn (Single Back Cross, SBC); rep from *, end p1.
Row 6—P1, * p1, SFC, BC, p2, FC, SBC, p1; rep from *, end p1.
Row 8—P1, * p2, sl 1 st to dpn and hold in back, k2, then k1-b from dpn (Back Knit Cross, BKC); p4; sl 2 sts to dpn and hold in front, k1-b, then k2 from dpn (Front Knit Cross, FKC); p2; rep from *, end p1.
Row 10—P1, * p1, BC, SFC, p2, SBC, FC, p1; rep from *, end p1.
Row 12—P1, * BC, p2, SFC, SBC, p2, FC; rep from *, end p1.
Row 14—P1, k2, * p4, sl 1 st to dpn and hold in back, k1-b, then k1-b from dpn; p4, sl 2 sts to dpn and hold in back, k2, then k2 from dpn; rep from * to last 3 sts, end last repeat k2, p1.
Row 16—P1, * FC, p2, SBC, SFC, p2, BC; rep from *, end p1.
Row 18—P1, * p1, FC, SBC, p2, SFC, BC, p1; rep from *, end p1.
Row 20—P1, * p2, FKC, p4, BKC, p2; rep from *, end p1.
Row 22—P1, * p1, SBC, FC, p2, BC, SFC, p1; rep from *, end p1.
Row 24—P1, * SBC, p2, FC, BC, p2, SFC; rep from *, end p1.

Repeat Rows 1–24.

89

Cluster Stitch

Cluster Stitch

In this pattern no stitches are cabled—that is, crossed over each other. But the work does require the use of a cable needle, and so Cluster Stitch is classified as a cable pattern.

Like Bobbles, a series of Clusters can be used as a fancy texture spot-pattern, as shown. Or, Clusters can be worked as a form of Smocking, to tie together various sizes of knit-purl ribs. (See Ribbed Cluster Diamond Pattern.) Larger Clusters can be made by winding the yarn more times; smaller ones by winding fewer times. The winding can be tight or loose, depending on whether the knitter wishes the clustered stitches squeezed together or not.

Multiple of 6 sts plus 5.

Row 1 (Wrong side) and all other wrong-side rows—Purl.
Row 2—Knit.
Row 4—K4, * knit next 3 sts and transfer the 3 sts just knitted onto dpn; then wind yarn 6 times counterclockwise (looking down from top) around these 3 sts under dpn; then return the 3 sts to right-hand needle (Cluster 3); k3; rep from *, end k1.
Row 6—Knit.
Row 8—K1, * Cluster 3, k3; rep from *, end Cluster 3, k1.

Repeat Rows 1–8.

The Anchor

The Anchor

Although this pattern is worked in a panel, it does not continue vertically but is completed, instead, at the end of 42 rows. It may, of course, be started again in the next panel above, or worked horizontally across the fabric by repeating the pattern every 32 stitches. Note that the Front Cross and Back Cross are made on both sides of the fabric to give a shallow slant to the traveling stitches.

Panel of 32 sts.

Row 1 (Right side)—Purl.
Row 2—Knit.
Row 3—P15, k2, p15.

90

Row 4—K15, p2, k15.

Row 5—P14, sl next st to dpn and hold in back, k1, then k1 from dpn; sl next st to dpn and hold in front, k1, then k1 from dpn; p14.

Row 6—K13, sl next st to dpn and hold in front, *p1*, then k1 from dpn (Front Cross, FC); p2; sl next st to dpn and hold in back, k1, then *p1* from dpn (Back Cross, BC); k13.

Row 7—P12, BC, p1, k2, p1, FC, p12.

Row 8—K11, FC, k2, p2, k2, BC, k11.

Row 9—P10, BC, p3, k2, p3, FC, p10.

Row 10—K9, FC, k4, p2, k4, BC, k9.

Row 11—P8, BC, p5, k2, p5, FC, p8.

Row 12—K7, FC, k6, p2, k6, BC, k7.

Row 13—P6, BC, p7, k2, p7, FC, p6.

Row 14—K5, FC, k8, p2, k8, BC, k5.

Row 15—P4, BC, p9, k2, p9, FC, p4.

Row 16—K1, p1, (k2, p1) twice, k7, p2, k7, (p1, k2) twice, p1, k1.

Row 17—P1, FC, p1, k1, p1, BC, p7, k2, p7, FC, p1, k1, p1, BC, p1.

Row 18—K2, (p1, k1) twice, p1, k8, p2, k8, (p1, k1) twice, p1, k2.

Row 19—P2, FC, k1, BC, p8, k2, p8, FC, k1, BC, p2.

Row 20—K3, p3, k9, p2, k9, p3, k3.

Row 21—P3, Make One (M1) purlwise by lifting running thread between the st just worked and the next st, and purling into the back of this thread; sl 1—k2 tog—psso, M1 purlwise, p9, k2, p9, M1 purlwise, sl 1—k2 tog—psso, M1 purlwise, p3.

Row 22—K4, p1, k10, p2, k10, p1, k4.

Row 23—P10, Make Bobble (MB) as follows: (k1, yo, k1, yo, k1) in next st, turn and p5; turn and k5; turn and p2 tog, p1, p2 tog; turn and sl 1—k2 tog—psso, completing Bobble; p4, k2, p4, MB, p10.

Row 24—K10, p1 b, k4, p2, k4, p1 b, k10.

Row 25—P10, FC, p3, k2, p3, BC, p10.

Row 26—K11, BC, k2, p2, k2, FC, k11.

Row 27—P12, FC, p1, k2, p1, BC, p12.

Row 28—K13, BC, p2, FC, k13.

Row 29—P14, FC, BC, p14.

Row 30—Repeat Row 4.

Row 31—P15, sl next st to dpn and hold in front, k1, then k1 from dpn; p15.

Row 32—K14, FC, BC, k14.

Row 33—P13, BC, p2, FC, p13.

Row 34—K12, FC, k4, BC, k12.

Row 35—P12, k1, p6, k1, p12.

Row 36—K12, p1, k6, p1, k12.

Row 37—P12, FC, p4, BC, p12.

Row 38—K13, BC, k2, FC, k13.

Row 39—P14, FC, BC, p14.

Row 40—K15, skip 1 st and purl the 2nd st, then purl the skipped st and sl both sts from needle together; k15.

Row 41—Purl.

Row 42—Knit.

Cable Chevron

Cable Chevron

This interesting fabric is the result of uniting a series of Double Cables all the way across a row. It looks about the same upside down or right side up—an advantage in some cases when a garment is being worked from the top down, or in an article like a pillow cover or baby blanket that can be turned either way.

Multiple of 12 sts plus 2.

Row 1 (Wrong side) and all other wrong-side rows—Purl.

Row 2—K1, * sl next 3 sts to dpn and hold in back, k3, then k3 from dpn; sl next 3 sts to dpn and hold in front, k3, then k3 from dpn; rep from *, end k1.

Rows, 4, 6, and 8—Knit.

Repeat Rows 1–8.

The Candle Tree

The Candle Tree

On Rows 9–21 of this pattern, cabled crossings are performed on both sides of the fabric to make the graceful spread of the Tree's lower "branches". The upper boughs hold nine Leaf or Candle-Flame motifs, all alike, in a very naturalistic tree-shaped arrangement. The entire panel with its 52 rows is a complete design, roughly square in shape. It may be used only once, as a central ornament in a garment, or it may be placed in blocks at any desired distance from each other. It is an ideal pattern for bedspreads and throws, since it can be made in squares of contrasting colors and the squares then sewn or crocheted together. To repeat the pattern as a vertical panel, work several rows of some other pattern as a horizontal band before beginning the next Candle Tree.

Panel of 35 sts.

NOTES: Front Purl Cross (FPC): sl 1 st to dpn and hold in front, p1, then k1 from dpn. Back Purl Cross (BPC): sl 1 st to dpn and hold in back, k1, then p1 from dpn.

Front Knit Cross (FKC): sl 1 st to dpn and hold in front, k1, then k1 from dpn.

Back Knit Cross (BKC): sl 1 st to dpn and hold in back, k1, then k1 from dpn.

Rows 1, 3, 5, and 7 (Right side)—P16 k3, p16.

Rows 2, 4, 6, and 8—K16, p3, k16.

Row 9—P15, BKC, k1, FKC, p15.

Row 10—K14, FPC, p3, BPC, k14.

Row 11—P13, BPC, p1, k3, p1, FPC, p13.

Row 12—K12, FPC, k2, p3, k2, BPC, k12.

Row 13—P11, BKC, p3, k3, p3, FKC, p11.

Row 14—K10, FPC, p1, k3, p3, k3, p1, BPC, k10.

Row 15—P9, BPC, p1, k1, p3, k3, p3, k1, p1, FPC, p9.

Row 16—K8, FPC, k2, p1, k3, p3, k3, p1, k2, BPC, k8.

Row 17—P7, BKC, p3, yo, k1, yo, p3, k3, p3, yo, k1, yo, p3, FKC, p7.

Row 18—K6, FPC, p1, (k3, p3) 3 times, k3, p1, BPC, k6.

Row 19—P5, BPC, p1, k1, p3, (k1, yo) twice, k1, p3, k3, p3, (k1, yo) twice, k1, p3, k1, p1, FPC, p5.

Row 20—K4, FPC, k2, p1, k3, p5, k3, p3, k3, p5, k3, p1, k2, BPC, k4.

Row 21—P3, BPC, p3, k1, p3, k2, yo, k1, yo, k2, p3, k3, p3, k2, yo, k1, yo, k2, p3, k1, p3, FPC, p3.

Row 22 and all subsequent wrong-side rows: Knit all knit sts and purl all purl and yo sts.

Row 23—P3, yo, k1, yo, p4, k1, p3, ssk, k3, k2 tog, p3, k3, p3, ssk, k3, k2 tog, p3, k1, p4, yo, k1, yo, p3.

Row 25—P3, (k1, yo) twice, k1, p4, k1, p3, ssk, k1, k2 tog, p3, k3, p3, ssk, k1, k2 tog, p3, k1, p4, (k1, yo) twice, k1, p3.

Row 27—P3, k2, yo, k1, yo, k2, p4, yo, k1, yo, p3, sl 1—k2 tog—psso, p2, BPC, k1, FPC, p2, sl 1—k2 tog—psso, p3, yo, k1, yo, p4, k2, yo, k1, yo, k2, p3.

Row 29—P3, ssk, k3, k2 tog, p4, (k1, yo) twice, k1, p5, BPC, p1, k1, p1, FPC, p5, (k1, yo) twice, k1, p4, ssk, k3, k2 tog, p3.

Row 31—P3, ssk, k1, k2 tog, p4, k2, yo, k1, yo, k2, p4, BPC, p2, k1, p2, FPC, p4, k2, yo, k1, yo, k2, p4, ssk, k1, k2 tog, p3.

Row 33—P3, sl 1—k2 tog—psso, p4, ssk, k3, k2 tog, p3, BPC, p3, k1, p3, FPC, p3, ssk, k3, k2 tog, p4, sl 1—k2 tog—psso, p3.

Row 35—P8, ssk, k1, k2 tog, p3, yo, k1, yo, p4, k1, p4, yo, k1, yo, p3, ssk, k1, k2 tog, p8.

Row 37—P8, sl 1—k2 tog—psso, p3, (k1, yo) twice, (k1, p4) twice, (k1, yo) twice, k1, p3, sl 1—k2 tog—psso, p8.

Row 39—P12, k2, yo, k1, yo, k2, p4, yo, k1, yo, p4, k2, yo, k1, yo, k2, p12.

Row 41—P12, ssk, k3, k2 tog, p4, (k1, yo) twice, k1, p4, ssk, k3, k2 tog, p12.

Row 43—P12, ssk, k1, k2 tog, p4, k2, yo, k1, yo, k2, p4, ssk, k1, k2 tog, p12.

Row 45—P12, sl 1—k2 tog—psso, p4, ssk, k3, k2 tog, p4, sl 1—k2 tog—psso, p12.

Row 47—P17, ssk, k1, k2 tog, p17.

Row 49—P17, sl 1—k2 tog—psso, p17.

Row 51—Purl.

Row 52 (Wrong side)—Knit.

Wave Lattice

This is a graceful "basketweave" pattern in which the left and right crosses alternate, which gives a wavy effect. On every other right-side row one set of ribs is "skipped" while the other set is being cabled.

Multiple of 6 sts plus 2.

Rows 1 and 3 (Wrong side)—K1, * k2, p4; rep from *, end k1.
Row 2—K1, * sl next 2 sts to dpn and hold in front, k2, then k2 from dpn; p2; rep from *, end k1.
Row 4—K1, p2, * k2, sl next 2 sts to dpn and hold in back, k2, then p2 from dpn; rep from *, end k5.
Rows 5 and 7—K1, * p4, k2; rep from *, end k1.
Row 6—K1, * p2, sl next 2 sts to dpn and hold in back, k2, then k2 from dpn; rep from *, end k1.
Row 8—K5, * sl next 2 sts to dpn and hold in front, p2, then k2 from dpn; k2; rep from *, end p2, k1.

Repeat Rows 1–8.

Wave Lattice

Two Variations on the Aran Honeycomb: Rings and Telescope Lattice

Both of these patterns contain portions of the classic Aran Honeycomb. Rings is a honeycomb with every other cell omitted; Telescope Lattice makes an allover pattern of the upper portions of the cells. Both make beautiful texture effects.

Notes: FC (Front Cross): Sl 2 sts to dpn and hold in front, k2, then k2 from dpn.

BC (Back Cross): Sl 2 sts to dpn and hold in back, k2, then k2 from dpn.

I. RINGS

Multiple of 16 sts plus 2.

Row 1 (Wrong side) and all other wrong-side rows—Purl.
Rows 2, 6, 10, and 14—Knit.
Row 4—K1, * k8, FC, BC; rep from *, end k1.
Row 8—K1, * BC, FC, k8; rep from *, end k1.
Row 12—K1, * FC, BC, k8; rep from *, end k1.
Row 16—K1, * k8, BC, FC; rep from *, end k1.

Repeat Rows 1–16.

Aran Honeycomb Variation I: Rings

II. TELESCOPE LATTICE

Multiple of 12 sts plus 2.

Row 1 (Wrong side) and all other wrong-side rows—Purl.
Rows 2 and 6—Knit.
Row 4—K1, * BC, k4, FC; rep from *, end k1.
Row 8—K1, * k2, FC, BC, k2; rep from *, end k1.

Repeat Rows 1–8.

Aran Honeycomb Variation II: Telescope Lattice

Rib and Braid Pattern

Tired of that dreary old "k2, p2" in a ribbed pullover? Try this beautiful contemporary German pattern instead! You'll have a much more interesting sweater, and enjoy working it.

Multiple of 18 sts plus 3.

NOTES: FC (Front Cross): sl 1 st to dpn and hold in front, p1, then k1 from dpn.
FKC (Front Knit Cross): same as FC, but knit both sts.
BC (Back Cross): sl 1 st to dpn and hold in back, k1, then p1 from dpn.
BKC (Back Knit Cross): same as BC, but knit both sts.

Rows 1 and 3 (Wrong side)—K3, * p2, k2, p2, k3; rep from *.
Row 2—P3, * BKC, p2, BKC, p3; rep from *.
Row 4—* P2, (BC, FC) twice, (p2, k2) twice; rep from *, end p3.
Rows 5 and 7—K3, * (p2, k2) twice, p1, k2, p2, k2, p1, k2; rep from *.
Row 6—* P2, k1, p2, FKC, p2, k1, (p2, k2) twice; rep from *, end p3.
Row 8—* P2, (FC, BC) twice, (p2, k2) twice; rep from *, end p3.
Row 9—Repeat first row.
Row 10—P3, * BKC, p2, BKC, p3, k2, p2, k2, p3; rep from *.
Rows 11 through 19—Repeat Rows 3 through 9, then repeat Rows 2 and 3 again.
Row 20—P3, * (k2, p2) twice, (BC, FC) twice, p2; rep from *.
Rows 21 and 23—* K2, p1, k2, p2, k2, p1, (k2, p2) twice; rep from *, end k3.
Row 22—P3, * (k2, p2) twice, k1, p2, FKC, p2, k1, p2; rep from *.
Row 24—P3, * (k2, p2) twice, (FC, BC) twice, p2; rep from *.
Rows 25 and 27—Repeat first row.
Row 26—P3, * k2, p2, k2, p3, BKC, p2, BKC, p3; rep from *.
Rows 28 through 32—Repeat Rows 20 through 24.

Repeat Rows 1–32.

Rib and Braid Pattern

Arcade Pattern

Arcade Pattern

Contributed by Bernice Haedike, Oak Park, Illinois

This can be worked in a single panel of 15 stitches, in which case it looks more like a type of double cable with bobbles than an "arcade" of pillars and arches. It is unusual and pretty, and makes a fascinating allover design rich with texture interest.

Multiple of 13 sts plus 2.

NOTES: Front Cross (FC): sl 2 sts to dpn and hold in front, p1, then k2 from dpn.

Back Cross (BC): sl 1 st to dpn and hold in back, k2, then p1 from dpn.

Row 1 (Wrong side)—Knit.

Row 2—K3, * p3, (k1, yo, k1, yo, k1) in next st, p1, (k1, yo, k1, yo, k1) in next st, p3, k4; rep from *, end last repeat k3.

Row 3—P3, * k3, p5, k1, p5, k3, p4; rep from *, end last repeat p3.

Row 4—K3, * p3, ssk, k1, k2 tog, p1, ssk, k1, k2 tog, p3, k4; rep from *, end last repeat k3.

Row 5—P3, * k3, p3 tog, k1, p3 tog, k3, p4; rep from *, end last repeat p3.

Row 6—K3, * p4, (k1, yo, k1, yo, k1) in next st, p4, k4; rep from *, end last repeat k3.

Row 7—P3, * k4, p5, k4, p4; rep from *, end last repeat p3.

Row 8—K1, * FC, p3, ssk, k1, k2 tog, p3, BC; rep from *, end k1.

Row 9—K2, * p2, k3, p3 tog, k3, p2, k2; rep from *.

Row 10—P2, * FC, p5, BC, p2; rep from *.

Row 11—K3, * p2, k5, p2, k4; rep from *, end last repeat k3.

Row 12—P3, * FC, p3, BC, p4; rep from *, end last repeat p3.

Row 13—K4, * p2, k3, p2, k6; rep from *, end last repeat k4.

Row 14—P4, * FC, p1, BC, p6; rep from *, end last repeat p4.

Row 15—K5, * p2, k1, p2, k8; rep from *, end last repeat k5.

Row 16—P5, * sl next 3 sts to dpn and hold in back, k2, then sl the purl st from dpn back to left-hand needle and purl it; then k2 from dpn; p8; rep from *, end last repeat p5.

Repeat Rows 1-16.

Sunburst Check Pattern

Contributed by Hildegard M. Elsner, Aldan, Pennsylvania

This beautiful pattern comes from Austria, and lends itself to a multitude of uses. It is informal enough for ski sweaters, yet disciplined enough for fascinatingly embossed coatings. It will also make delightful afghans and baby blankets.

Multiple of 12 sts plus 2.

NOTES: Front Cross (FC)—sl 1 st to dpn and hold in front, p3, then k1 from dpn.

Back Cross (BC)—sl 3 sts to dpn and hold in back, k1, then p3 from dpn.

Row 1 (Right side)—K4, * p6, k6; rep from *, end p6, k4.
Row 2—P1, * k6, p6; rep from *, end k6, p1.
Row 3—K3, * FC, BC, k4; rep from *, end last repeat k3.
Row 4—P3, * k3, p2, k3, p4; rep from *, end last repeat p3.
Row 5—K2, * FC, k2, BC, k2; rep from *.
Row 6—P2, * k3, p4, k3, p2; rep from *.
Row 7—K1, * FC, k4, BC; rep from *, end k1.
Rows 8, 10, and 12—Repeat Row 1.
Rows 9 and 11—Repeat Row 2.
Row 13—K1, * BC, k4, FC; rep from *, end k1.
Rows 14, 16, and 18—Repeat Rows 6, 4, and 2.
Row 15—K2, * BC, k2, FC, k2; rep from *.
Row 17—K3, * BC, FC, k4; rep from *, end last repeat k3.
Rows 19 and 20—Repeat Rows 1 and 2.

Repeat Rows 1–20.

Sunburst Check Pattern

Two Cable-and-Texture Patterns: Sidecurl Pattern and Marrowbone Pattern

I. SIDECURL PATTERN

Simple cables are repeated across this fabric; the novel touch is given by small purled blocks which appear to continue the curve of the cable off to one side. This is an easy-to work pattern that makes a firm, thick fabric.

Multiple of 6 sts plus 2.

Rows 1 and 3 (Wrong side)—Purl.
Rows 2 and 4—Knit.
Row 5—K2, * p4, k2; rep from *.
Row 6—P2, * sl next 2 sts to dpn and hold in front, k2, then k2 from dpn; p2; rep from *.

Repeat Rows 1–6.

ABOVE: *Sidecurl Pattern*
BELOW: *Marrowbone Pattern*

II. MARROWBONE PATTERN

A beautiful variation on the cabled honeycomb is made here by stitches cabled in one direction only, while the other diagonals are formed of garter stitch. This pattern makes fine, sturdy afghans and sweaters in a non-curling fabric.

Multiple of 12 sts plus 4.

NOTE: Front Cross (FC): sl 3 sts to dpn and hold in front, k3, then k3 from dpn.

Rows 1 and 3 (Right side)—Knit.
Row 2—* P6, k6; rep from *, end p4.
Row 4—K2, * p6, k6; rep from *, end p2.
Row 5—K2, * k6, FC; rep from *, end k2.
Row 6—K4, * p6, k6; rep from *.
Rows 7 and 9—Knit.
Row 8—* K6, p6; rep from *, end k4.
Row 10—P2, * k6, p6; rep from *, end k2.
Row 11—K2, * FC, k6; rep from *, end k2.
Row 12—P4, * k6, p6; rep from *.

Repeat Rows 1–12.

Mutton-Chop Cables

Mutton-Chop Cables

Contributed by Hildegard M. Elsner, Aldan, Pennsylvania

These cables are Tyrolean, seen in ski sweaters. They are handsome in a single panel of 22 stitches, or as an allover pattern as given.

Multiple of 20 sts plus 2.

Rows 1 and 3 (Wrong side)—K2, * p8, k2; rep from *.
Row 2—K10, * p2, k18; rep from *, end last repeat k10.
Row 4—K2, * sl next 4 sts to dpn and hold in back, p4, then k4 from dpn; p2, sl next 4 sts to dpn and hold in front, k4, then p4 from dpn; k2; rep from *.
Rows 5 and 7—K6, * p4, k2, p4, k10; rep from *, end last repeat k6.
Row 6—K2, * p4, k4, p2, k4, p4, k2; rep from *.
Row 8—Repeat Row 2.
Row 9—Repeat Row 1.
Row 10—Repeat Row 2.

Repeat Rows 1–10.

Fancy Cable Check

In this pattern, small simple cables are placed to good advantage in a textured knit-purl fabric. Many slightly different arrangements are possible, but this one is typical. It makes excellent sport sweaters, blankets, throws, etc.

Multiple of 18 sts plus 1.

NOTE. Back Cross (BC): sl 3 sts to dpn and hold in back, k3, then k3 from dpn.

Row 1 (Right side)—K1, * p8, k1, p1, k6, p1, k1; rep from *.
Row 2—P1, * k1, p6, k1, p1, k8, p1; rep from *.
Row 3—K2, * p6, k2, p1, BC, p1, k2; rep from *, end last repeat k1.
Row 4—P1, * k1, p6, k1, p2, k6, p2; rep from *.
Row 5—K3, * p4, k3, p1, k6, p1, k3; rep from *, end last repeat k1.
Row 6—P1, * k1, p6, k1, p3, k4, p3; rep from *.
Row 7—K4, * p2, k4, p1, k6, p1, k4; rep from *, end last repeat k1.
Row 8—P1, * k1, p6, k1, p4, k2, p4; rep from *.
Row 9—* K10, p1, BC, p1; rep from *, end k1.
Rows 10 through 17—Repeat Rows 8, 7, 6, 5, 4, 3, 2, and 1.
Row 18—P1, * k1, p6, k1, p1; rep from *.
Row 19—K1, * p1, k6, p1, k1, p8, k1; rep from *.
Row 20—P1, * k8, p1, k1, p6, k1, p1; rep from *.
Row 21—K1, * p1, BC, p1, k2, p6, k2; rep from *.
Row 22—P2, * k6, p2, k1, p6, k1, p2; rep from *, end last repeat p1.
Row 23—K1, * p1, k6, p1, k3, p4, k3; rep from *.
Row 24—P3, * k4, p3, k1, p6, k1, p3; rep from *, end last repeat p1.
Row 25—K1, * p1, k6, p1, k4, p2, k4; rep from *.
Row 26—P4, * k2, p4, k1, p6, k1, p4; rep from *, end last repeat p1.
Row 27—K1, * p1, BC, p1, k10; rep from *.
Rows 28 through 36—Repeat Rows 26, 25, 24, 23, 22, 21, 20, 19, and 18.

Repeat Rows 1–36.

Fancy Cable Check

Cable and Ladder

Multiple of 14 sts plus 1.

Row 1 (Wrong side) and all other wrong-side rows—K1, * p2 tog, yo, p11, k1; rep from *.
Row 2—K1, * ssk, yo, sl next 3 sts to dpn and hold in back, k3, then k3 from dpn; k6; rep from *.
Row 4—K1, * ssk, yo, k12; rep from *.
Row 6—K1, * ssk, yo, k3, sl next 3 sts to dpn and hold in front, k3, then k3 from dpn; k3; rep from *.
Row 8—Repeat Row 4.

Repeat Rows 1–8.

Cable and Ladder

Knotted Lattice

Knotted Lattice

This handsome allover pattern has two-stitch ribs twisted, interlaced, curled around each other, and "traveled" diagonally across the fabric. It can be used in a panel of 20 stitches, but appears more intricate and interesting with more repeats.

Multiple of 12 sts plus 8.

Notes: Front Cross (FC): sl 2 sts to dpn and hold in front, k2, then k2 from dpn.

Back Cross (BC): sl 2 sts to dpn and hold in back, k2, then k2 from dpn.

Single Front Cross (SFC): sl 2 sts to dpn and hold in front, p1, then k2 from dpn.

Single Back Cross (SBC): sl 1 st to dpn and hold in back, k2, then p1 from dpn.

Rows 1, 3, 5, 7, 9, and 11 (Wrong side)—K1, * p6, k2, p2, k2; rep from *, end p6, k1.

Row 2—K1, * BC, (k2, p2) twice; rep from *, end BC, k3.

Row 4—K3, * FC, p2, RT, p2, k2; rep from *, end FC, k1.

Row 6—K7, * p2, k2, p2, k6; rep from *, end k1.

Row 8—K1, * BC, k2, p2, RT, p2; rep from *, end BC, k3.

Row 10—K3, * FC, (p2, k2) twice; rep from *, end FC, k1.

Row 12—K1, p2, * k2, SFC, p1, RT, p1, SBC; rep from *, end k2, p2, k1.

Row 13—K3, * p2, k1; rep from *, end k2.

Row 14—K1, p2, * RT, p1, SFC, k2, SBC, p1; rep from *, end RT, p2, k1.

Rows 15, 17, 19, 21, 23, and 25—K3, * p2, k2, p6, k2; rep from *, end p2, k3.

Row 16—K1, p2, k2, p2, * BC, (k2, p2) twice; rep from *, end k1.

Row 18—K1, * p2, RT, p2, k2, FC; rep from *, end p2, RT, p2, k1.

Row 20—K1, * p2, k2, p2, k6; rep from *, end p2, k2, p2, k1.

Row 22—K1, * p2, RT, p2, BC, k2; rep from *, end p2, RT, p2, k1.

Row 24—K1, * (p2, k2) twice, FC; rep from *, end p2, k2, p2, k1.

Row 26—K1, p2, * RT, p1, SBC, k2, SFC, p1; rep from *, end RT, p2, k1.

Row 27—Repeat Row 13.

Row 28—K1, p2, * k2, SBC, p1, RT, p1, SFC; rep from *, end k2, p2, k1.

Repeat Rows 1–28.

Double-Knotted Lattice

This beautiful design will make the best "bold-and-bulky" sweater you ever saw! One of the finest of the heavy-lattice patterns, it has an aura of foursquare solidity. A single panel, 30 stitches wide, also makes an excellent cable.

Notice that although the four-stitch clusters made in Rows 14 and 28 can't be seen, they do serve a purpose. The stitches gathered together by these clusters form a tight base for the double knots worked in subsequent rows.

Multiple of 16 sts plus 14.

NOTES: FC, BC, SFC, and SBC—same as for Knotted Lattice.

Cluster 4 as follows (worked from wrong side): sl 4 wyib, pass yarn to front, sl the same 4 sts back to left-hand needle, pass yarn to back, sl 4 wyib again.

Row 1 (Right side)—P3, * FC, BC, p8; rep from *, end last repeat p3.

Rows 2 and 4—K3, * p8, k8; rep from *, end last repeat k3.

Row 3—P3, * k8, p8; rep from *, end last repeat p3.

Rows 5, 6, 7, 8, and 9—Repeat Rows 1 through 4, then Row 1 again.

Row 10—K3, * p2, Cluster 4, p2, k8; rep from *, end last repeat k3.

Row 11—P2, * SBC, p4, SFC, p6; rep from *, end last repeat p2.

Row 12—K2, * p2, k6; rep from *, end last repeat k2.

Row 13—P1, * SBC, p6, SFC, p4; rep from *, end last repeat p1.

Row 14—K1, p2, * k8, p2, Cluster 4, p2; rep from *, end k8, p2, k1.

Row 15—P1, k2, * p8, FC, BC; rep from *, end p8, k2, p1.

Rows 16 and 18—K1, p2, * k8, p8; rep from *, end k8, p2, k1.

Row 17—P1, k2, * p8, k8; rep from *, end p8, k2, p1.

Rows 19, 20, 21, 22, and 23—Repeat Rows 15 through 18, then Row 15 again.

Row 24—Repeat Row 14.

Row 25—P1, * SFC, p6, SBC, p4; rep from *, end last repeat p1.

Row 26—Repeat Row 12.

Row 27—P2, * SFC, p4, SBC, p6; rep from *, end last repeat p2.

Row 28—Repeat Row 10.

Repeat Rows 1–28.

Double-Knotted Lattice

Tudor Grillwork

A clever trick enables this lovely pattern to maintain the same fabric width throughout both the straight rib rows and the cabled rows. Ordinarily the latter would "draw in" more; but the increases made invisibly in Row 8 allow greater leeway for crossing the stitches. Another clever trick, that of twisting the straight ribs on every right-side row, gives a uniform depth and roundness to all the pattern lines, both vertical and diagonal.

Tudor Grillwork also makes a beautiful cable when used in a panel of 22 or 32 stitches.

Multiple of 10 sts plus 2.

NOTES: Front Cross (FC)—sl 2 sts to dpn and hold in front, p2, then k2 from dpn.

Tudor Grillwork

Back Cross (BC)—sl 2 sts to dpn and hold in back, k2, then p2 from dpn.

Back Knit Cross (BKC)—sl 2 sts to dpn and hold in back, k2, then k2 from dpn.

Rows 1, 3, 5, and 7 (Right side)—P5, * RT, p8; rep from *, end RT, p5.

Rows 2, 4, and 6—K5, * p2, k8; rep from *, end p2, k5.

Row 8—K5, * purl into the front and back of each of the next 2 sts, k8; rep from *, end last repeat k5.

Row 9—P5, * BKC, p8; rep from *, end last repeat p5.

Row 10—K5, * p4, k8; rep from *, end p4, k5.

Row 11—P3, * BC, FC, p4; rep from *, end last repeat p3.

Row 12—K3, * p2, k4; rep from *, end p2, k3.

Row 13—P1, * BC, p4, FC; rep from *, end p1.

Row 14—K1, p2, * k8, p4; rep from *, end k8, p2, k1.

Row 15—P1, k2, * p8, BKC; rep from *, end p8, k2, p1.

Rows 16 and 18—Repeat Rows 14 and 12.

Row 17—P1, * FC, p4, BC; rep from *, end p1.

Row 19—P3, * FC, BC, p4; rep from *, end last repeat p3.

Row 20—K5, * (p2 tog) twice, k8; rep from *, end last repeat k5.

Repeat Rows 1–20.

Cherry Tree

Cherry Tree

This is a handsome allover pattern of cabling and openwork, which could be used in a single panel of 19 stitches. It makes a very attractive fine-yarn sweater, a baby's dress, or a stole.

Multiple of 18 sts plus 1.

NOTES: Front Cross (FC): sl 1 st to dpn and hold in front, p2, then k1 from dpn.

Back Cross (BC): sl 2 sts to dpn and hold in back, k1, then p2 from dpn.

Row 1 (Wrong side)—K1, * p6, k5, p6, k1; rep from *.

Row 2—P1, * k3, BC, p5, FC, k3, p1; rep from *.

Row 3—K1, * p4, k9, p4, k1; rep from *.

Row 4—P1, * FC, k1, p1, (yo, p2 tog) 4 times, k1, BC, p1; rep from *.

Row 5—K3, * p6, k1, p6, k5; rep from *, end last repeat k3.

Row 6—P3, * FC, k3, p1, k3, BC, p5; rep from *, end last repeat p3.

Row 7—K5, * p4, k1, p4, k9; rep from *, end last repeat k5.

Row 8—P1, * (yo, p2 tog) twice, k1, BC, p1, FC, k1, p1, (yo, p2 tog) twice; rep from *.

Repeat Rows 1–8.

Exchange Cables

Planning to make a sweater with little cables all over? Use this charming pattern instead of all those endless rows of plain cables—you'll be glad you did. Each cable exchanges ribs with its neighbor at intervals, thus creating a far more interesting design.

And here's another sort of exchange, to work a variation that you can discover for yourself. Throughout the pattern, exchange the positions of "FC" and "BC"—working "FC" in place of every "BC", and vice versa—leaving all other directions the same. The result will surprise you!

For a test swatch, cast on a minimum of 32 sts.

Exchange Cables

Multiple of 16 sts.

NOTES: Front Cross (FC)—sl 2 sts to dpn and hold in front, k2, then k2 from dpn.

Front Purl Cross (FPC)—sl 2 sts to dpn and hold in front, p2, then k2 from dpn.

Single Front Cross (SFC)—sl 2 sts to dpn and hold in front, p1, then k2 from dpn.

Back Cross (BC)—sl 2 sts to dpn and hold in back, k2, then k2 from dpn.

Back Purl Cross (BPC)—sl 2 sts to dpn and hold in back, k2, then p2 from dpn.

Single Back Cross (SBC)—sl 1 st to dpn and hold in back, k2, then p1 from dpn.

Rows 1, 3, 5, 7, 9, and 11 (Wrong side)—K2, * p4, k4; rep from *, end p4, k2.

Rows 2, 6, and 10—P2, * FC, p4, BC, p4; rep from *, end last repeat p2.

Rows 4 and 8—P2, * k4, p4; rep from *, end k4, p2.

Row 12—P1, * SBC, FPC, BPC, SFC, p2; rep from *, end last repeat p1.

Rows 13 and 15—K1, * p2, k3, p4, k3, p2, k2; rep from *, end last repeat k1.

Row 14—P1, * k2, p3, BC, p3, k2, p2; rep from *, end last repeat p1.

Row 16—P1, * SFC, BPC, FPC, SBC, p2; rep from *, end last repeat p1.

Rows 17, 19, 21, 23, 25, and 27—Repeat odd-numbered rows 1 through 11.

Rows 18, 22, and 26—P2, * BC, p4, FC, p4; rep from *, end last repeat p2.

Rows 20 and 24—Repeat Rows 4 and 8.

Row 28—P1, SBC, SFC, * p2, SBC, FPC, BPC, SFC; rep from *, end p2, SBC, SFC, p1.

Rows 29 and 31—K1, (p2, k2) twice, * p2, k3, p4, k3, p2, k2; rep from *, end p2, k2, p2, k1.

Row 30—P1, (k2, p2) twice, * k2, p3, FC, p3, k2, p2; rep from *, end k2, p2, k2, p1.

Row 32—P1, SFC, SBC, * p2, SFC, BPC, FPC, SBC; rep from *, end p2, SFC, SBC, p1.

Repeat Rows 1–32.

Tilting Ladder Pattern

Tilting Ladder Pattern

In this utterly delightful fabric, a very clever use is made of the natural bias tendency of a lace trellis. The "ladders" seem to career at dangerous angles all through the pattern, but they are in fact quite well disciplined as far as knitting technique is concerned. Tilting Ladder Pattern is gay and fascinating in any kind of yarn, for any kind of garment.

Multiple of 13 sts plus 2.

Row 1 (Wrong side)—K2, * p5, k1, p5, k2; rep from *.
Row 2—P2, * k1, (yo, k2 tog) twice, p1, k5, p2; rep from *.
Rows 3 and 5—K2, * p4, k2, p5, k2; rep from *.
Row 4—P2, * k1, (yo, k2 tog) twice, p2, k4, p2; rep from *.
Row 6—P2, * k1, (yo, k2 tog) twice, p2, sl next 2 sts to dpn and hold in back, k2, then k2 from dpn, p2; rep from *.
Rows 7, 8, 9, 10, 11, and 12—Repeat Rows 3, 4, 5, and 6, then Rows 3 and 4 again.
Row 13—Repeat Row 1.
Row 14—P2, * k5, p1, (ssk, yo) twice, k1, p2; rep from *.
Rows 15 and 17—K2, * p5, k2, p4, k2; rep from *.
Row 16—P2, * k4, p2, (ssk, yo) twice, k1, p2; rep from *.
Row 18—P2, * sl next 2 sts to dpn and hold in front, k2, then k2 from dpn; p2, (ssk, yo) twice, k1, p2; rep from *.
Rows 19, 20, 21, 22, 23, and 24—Repeat Rows 15, 16, 17, and 18, then Rows 15 and 16 again.

Repeat Rows 1–24.

Crossed Banners

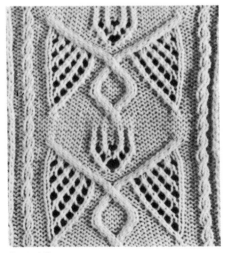

Crossed Banners

Two lacework flags topped by a small crown make an exceedingly elegant design for panel-, band-, or spot-pattern treatment. The small mock cables at the sides may be omitted, along with the edge stitches beyond them; this would leave a panel of 32 stitches. To conclude a single pattern used only once, work Rows 1 through 32 and then Rows 1, 2, and 3 again.

Panel of 40 sts.

NOTES: Front Cross (FC)—sl 2 sts to dpn and hold in front, p2, then k2 from dpn.

Back Cross (BC)—sl 2 sts to dpn and hold in back, k2, then p2 from dpn.

Front Knit Cross (FKC)—same as Front Cross, but *knit* all 4 sts.

Row 1 (Right side)—P2, k2, p32, k2, p2.

Row 2—K2, p2, k32, p2, k2.

Row 3—P2, RT, p32, RT, p2.

Rows 4 and 6—K2, p2, k3, p2, k9, p4, k9, p2, k3, p2, k2.

Row 5—P2, k2, p3, LT, p9, FKC, p9, RT, p3, k2, p2.

Row 7—P2, RT, p3, k1, yo, ssk, p6, BC, FC, p6, k2 tog, yo, k1, p3, RT, p2.

Rows 8, 10, 12, 14, 16, 18, and 20—Knit all knit sts, purl all purl and yo sts.

Row 9—P2, k2, p3, k2, yo, ssk, p3, BC, p4, FC, p3, k2 tog, yo, k2, p3, k2, p2.

Row 11—P2, RT, p3, k1, (yo, ssk) twice, p2, k2, p8, k2, p2, (k2 tog, yo) twice, k1, p3, RT, p2.

Row 13—P2, k2, p3, k2, (yo, ssk) twice, p1, FC, p4, BC, p1, (k2 tog, yo) twice, k2, p3, k2, p2.

Row 15—P2, RT, p3, k1, (yo, ssk) 3 times, p2, FC, BC, p2, (k2 tog, yo) 3 times, k1, p3, RT, p2.

Row 17—P2, k2, p3, k2, (yo, ssk) 3 times, p3, FKC, p3, (k2 tog, yo) 3 times, k2, p3, k2, p2.

Row 19—P2, RT, p3, k1, (yo, ssk) 4 times, BC, FC, (k2 tog, yo) 4 times, k1, p3, RT, p2.

Row 21—P2, k2, p3, k2, (yo, ssk) twice, k1, BC, p4, FC, k1, (k2 tog, yo) twice, k2, p3, k2, p2.

Row 22—K2, p2, (k3, p9, k3, p2) twice, k2.

Row 23—P2, RT, p3, k1, (yo, ssk) twice, BC, p2, k2 tog, (yo) twice, ssk, p2, FC, (k2 tog, yo) twice, k1, p3, RT, p2.

Row 24—K2, p2, k3, p7, k4, p1, (k1, p1) into the double yo, p1, k4, p7, k3, p2, k2.

Row 25—P2, k2, p3, k3, BC, p3, k2 tog, yo, k2, yo, ssk, p3, FC, k3, p3, k2, p2.

Row 26—K2, p2, k3, p5, k5, p6, k5, p5, k3, p2, k2.

Row 27—P2, RT, p3, k1, BC, p4, (k2 tog, yo) twice, (yo, ssk) twice [note: this makes a double yo at center], p4, FC, k1, p3, RT, p2.

Row 28—K2, p2, k3, p3, k6, p3, (k1, p1) into the double yo, p3, k6, p3, k3, p2, k2.

Row 29—P2, k2, p2, BC, p6, (k1-b, p1) twice, (p1, k1-b) twice, p6, FC, p2, k2, p2.

Row 30—K2, p2, k12, (p1-b, k1) twice, (k1, p1-b) twice, k12, p2, k2.

Row 31—P2, RT, p12, (k1-b, p1) twice, (p1, k1-b) twice, p12, RT, p2.

Row 32—Repeat Row 30.

Repeat Rows 1–32.

Cabled Feather Pattern

Contributed by Leona Hughes, Sarasota, Florida

Nearly all the best innovations in knitting are brought about by a simple association of ideas—like this one. Who, other than Mrs. Hughes, ever thought of putting a cable into Feather and Fan Stitch before? The idea is a thoroughly happy one, and the result is beautiful. The cables deepen the scallops, and emphasize the lace.

Cabled Feather Pattern

Wave cables could be used as well as simple cables, by crossing the stitches in front on every alternate cable row. For the larger version of Feather and Fan Stitch that is worked on multiples of 24 (8 decreases, 8 yo's), simply cross 4 stitches over 4. For a test swatch of this pattern, cast on a *minimum* of 36 stitches.

Multiple of 18 sts.

Row 1 (Wrong side)—Purl.

Row 2— * (K2 tog) 3 times, (yo, k1) 6 times, (k2 tog) 3 times; rep from *.

Row 3—K15, * p6, k12; rep from *, end k3.

Row 4—K15, * sl next 3 sts to dpn and hold in back, k3, then k3 from dpn; k12; rep from *, end k3.

Rows 5, 6, and 7—Repeat Rows 1, 2, and 3.

Row 8—Knit.

Repeat Rows 1–8.

Lace Lozenges

Lace Lozenges

An interesting "twist" of the cable needle is employed in this pattern to make an eight-stitch cross—or rather, to cross the two outside stitches in front of the intervening six. The rows are repetitive, and so are not given in consecutive order; but it is easy to see that there are four central yo's and three lateral ones, alternately, in each lozenge.

Multiple of 18 sts plus 1.

Rows 1, 5, 9, and 13 (Wrong side)—K1, * p1, k1, p4, k1, p1, k1; rep from *.

Rows 2, 6, 10, and 14—P1, * k1, p1, k2 tog, (yo) twice, ssk, p1, k1, p1; rep from *.

Rows 3, 7, 11, and 15—K1, * p1, k1, p1, (k1, p1) into the double yo of previous row, (p1, k1) twice; rep from *.

Rows 4 and 12—P1, * k1, p1, yo, k2 tog, ssk, yo, p1, k1, p1; rep from *.

Row 8—P1, * cross next 8 sts as follows: sl next st to dpn and hold in front, sl next 6 sts to right-hand needle, sl next st to dpn and hold in front, sl the same 6 sts back to left-hand needle; then twist dpn a half-turn counterclockwise, thus reversing positions of the 2 sts on it; then k1 from dpn; then p1, k4, p1; then knit the last st from dpn (8 sts crossed); p1, k1, p1, yo, k2 tog, ssk, yo, p1, k1, p1; rep from *.

Row 16— * P1, k1, p1, yo, k2 tog, ssk, yo, p1, k1, p1, cross next 8 sts as in Row 8; rep from *, end p1.

Repeat Rows 1–16.

3

Twist-Stitch Patterns

The standard method of working a Right Twist is: skip 1 st, knit the second st, then knit the skipped st and sl both sts from needle together. The standard method of working a Left Twist is: skip 1 st and knit the second st in back loop, then knit the skipped st in front loop and sl both sts from needle together.

These methods, however, are not "standard" in this book. Both twists can be done in a better way—at least, in this author's opinion. Your opinion may differ; so if you prefer to stick to the standard methods, by all means do so. But first, do consult the Glossary of this book and try out the directions given for "RT" and "LT". If you like these newer methods, use them; if not, ignore them henceforth. For most knitters they *will* produce a somewhat neater result than the old standard methods, and are perhaps a little faster to work.

Some of the patterns in this section employ still other methods of twisting stitches, and in these cases the method is explained in the pattern notes. Even the old standard methods, as above, are explained wherever they are used. But where "RT" and "LT" occur in any pattern *without* specific twist directions, then the methods intended are the ones described in the Glossary.

Having settled all that, we can proceed to a discussion of twist patterns in general. Very interesting patterns they are, too. Twist stitches constitute an excellent way of making "traveling" diagonal lines and cable-like panels, without any fussing with a cable needle. Twist stitches therefore can be adapted to all sorts of designs and shapes and backgrounds. It is easy to invent original twist patterns for yourself, because the basic technique is simple and can be used to make diagonal lines go in any direction and for any distance. The patterns that are given here in the panel form are so close to cables that they can be used at will as substitutes for cables or in combination with them. You can even make an entire fisherman sweater without ever using a cable needle, simply by planning the sweater all in twist-stitch panels!

When you work with twist stitches, your gauge is likely to have more stitches to the inch than stockinette stitch in the same yarn on the same needles. Twists pull the fabric together laterally, so you must be sure to cast on enough stitches for the proper width. Twist patterns work well in any kind of yarn, from heavy to fine; but the needles must not be too large in proportion to the weight of the yarn, because a twist worked with over-large needles will "open up" the stitches and leave them looking limp and sloppy.

Twist-stitch patterns can be simple or complex, sporty or dressy, picturesque or elegant. They are not confined to any particular type of yarn or style of knitwear. You can use them in dress-up coats or sport jackets, ski sweaters or cocktail dresses, children's wear or afghans. Choose a few that you like, and try them. Put them together with other kinds of patterns for contrast. Little ideas that lead on to big ones abound in knitting patterns, and the twist stitch is certainly one of the best of these little ideas.

Purl-Twist Knot

Purl-Twist Knot

Contributed by Helen R. McShane, Brooklyn, New York

This is an easy pattern that gives a pretty, nubby allover texture for coats and suits, sweaters, dresses, etc. The wrong side is interesting too as a rough purl fabric with a hint of a design.

Multiple of 4 sts.

Rows 1 and 3 (Wrong side)—Purl.
Row 2—* K2, p2 tog and leave on needle; insert right-hand needle from back between the sts just purled tog, and purl the first st again; then sl both sts from needle together; rep from *.
Row 4—* P2 tog and purl first st again (as in Row 2), k2; rep from *.

Repeat Rows 1–4.

Little Wave

Little Wave

Contributed by Eugen K. Beugler, Dexter, Oregon

Multiple of 6 sts plus 1.

Row 1 (Right side)—Knit.
Row 2—P2, * k2, p4; rep from *, end k2, p3.
Row 3—K2, * LT, k4; rep from *, end LT, k3.
Row 4—P2, * k1, p1, k1, p3; rep from *, end last repeat p2.
Row 5—K3, * LT, k4; rep from *, end LT, k2.
Row 6—P3, * k2, p4; rep from *, end k2, p2.
Row 7—Knit.
Rows 8 and 10—Repeat Rows 6 and 4.
Row 9—K3, * RT, k4; rep from *, end RT, k2.
Row 11—K2, * RT, k4; rep from *, end RT, k3.
Row 12—Repeat Row 2.

Repeat Rows 1–12.

Grain of Wheat

Contributed by Hildegard M. Elsner, Aldan, Pennsylvania

Multiple of 4 sts.

Row 1 (Wrong side)—Purl.
Row 2—K1, p2, * skip 1 st and knit into the *back* of second st, then knit the skipped st, then sl both sts from needle together (Left Twist); p2; rep from *, end k1.
Row 3—K3, * p2, k2; rep from *, end k1.
Row 4—K3, * skip 1 st and knit into the *front* of second st, then knit the skipped st, then sl both sts from needle together (Right Twist); k2; rep from *, end k1.
Row 5—Purl.
Row 6—K1, * Left Twist, p2; rep from *, end Left Twist, k1.
Row 7—K1, p2, * k2, p2; rep from *, end k1.
Row 8—K1, * Right Twist, k2; rep from *, end Right Twist, k1.

Repeat Rows 1–8.

Grain of Wheat

Branching Rib Pattern

Multiple of 8 sts plus 4.

Rows 1, 3, and 5 (Wrong side)—K1, p3, * k5, p3; rep from *.
Row 2—* LT, k1, p5; rep from *, end LT, k1, p1.
Row 4—* K1, LT, p5; rep from *, end k1, LT, p1.
Row 6—P1, * k2, p4, RT; rep from *, end k2, p1.
Row 7—K1, * p2, k1, p1, k4; rep from *, end p2, k1.
Row 8—P1, * k2, p3, RT, p1; rep from *, end k2, p1.
Row 9—K1, * p2, k2, p1, k3; rep from *, end p2, k1.
Row 10—P1, * k2, p2, RT, p2; rep from *, end k2, p1.
Row 11—K1, * p2, k3, p1, k2; rep from *, end p2, k1.
Row 12—P1, * k2, p1, RT, p3; rep from *, end k2, p1.
Row 13—K1, * p2, k4, p1, k1; rep from *, end p2, k1.
Row 14—P1, * k2, RT, p4; rep from *, end k2, p1.
Rows 15, 17, and 19—* P3, k5; rep from *, end p3, k1.
Row 16—P1, * k1, RT, p5; rep from *, end k1, RT.
Row 18—P1, * RT, k1, p5; rep from *, end RT, k1.
Row 20—P1, * k2, LT, p4; rep from *, end k2, p1.
Rows 21, 23, 25, and 27—Repeat Rows 13, 11, 9, and 7.
Row 22—P1, * k2, p1, LT, p3; rep from *, end k2, p1.
Row 24—P1, * k2, p2, LT, p2; rep from *, end k2, p1.
Row 26—P1, * k2, p3, LT, p1; rep from *, end k2, p1.
Row 28—P1, * k2, p4, LT; rep from *, end k2, p1.

Repeat Rows 1–28.

Branching Rib Pattern

Austrian Block Pattern

Contributed by Hildegard M. Elsner, Aldan, Pennsylvania

Austrian Block Pattern

Left unpressed, this simple but effective pattern closes up into deep ribs that are alternately broadened into leaf-like shapes and slimmed down to a single stitch. Because of this interesting texture, the pattern is good for bulky sweaters, and works beautifully in panels of 21 or 31 stitches.

Multiple of 10 sts plus 1.

Rows 1, 3, 5, 7, and 9 (Wrong side)—P1, * k2, p5, k2, p1; rep from *.

Rows 2, 4, 6, 8, and 10—K1-b, * p2, RT, k1, LT, p2, k1-b; rep from *.

Rows 11, 13, 15, 17, and 19—P3, * k2, p1, k2, p5; rep from *, end last repeat p3.

Rows 12, 14, 16, 18, and 20—K1, * LT, p2, k1-b, p2, RT, k1; rep from *.

Repeat Rows 1–20.

Wickerwork Pattern

Contributed by Hildegard M. Elsner, Aldan, Pennsylvania

Wickerwork Pattern

Multiple of 8 sts.

Row 1 (Wrong side)—P1, * k2, p2; rep from *, end k2, p1.
Row 2—* K1, p1, RT, LT, p1, k1; rep from *.
Row 3—* P1, k1, p1, k2, p1, k1, p1; rep from *.
Row 4—* K1, RT, p2, LT, k1; rep from *.
Row 5—P2, * k4, p4; rep from *, end k4, p2.
Row 6—Knit.
Row 7—Repeat Row 1.
Row 8—* LT, p1, k2, p1, RT; rep from *.
Row 9—* K1, p1, k1, p2, k1, p1, k1; rep from *.
Row 10—* P1, LT, k2, RT, p1; rep from *.
Row 11—K2, * p4, k4; rep from *, end p4, k2.
Row 12—Knit.

Repeat Rows 1–12.

Twisted Diagonal Stripe

This neat and subtle fabric looks like the impossible accomplished—diagonal bands of ribbing on a knit-stitch background! Of course, it isn't real ribbing, just twisted stitches. The same pattern can be done equally well with right twists; but in this case, the diagonals must be moved one stitch to the *left* on every right-side row, instead of to the right as given.

Twisted Diagonal Stripe

Multiple of 9 sts plus 3.

Row 1 (Wrong side) and all other wrong-side rows—Purl.
Row 2—K3, * (LT) 3 times, k3; rep from *.
Row 4—K2, * (LT) 3 times, k3; rep from *, end k1.
Row 6—K1, * (LT) 3 times, k3; rep from *, end LT.
Row 8—* (LT) 3 times, k3; rep from *, end LT, k1.
Row 10—K1, (LT) twice, * k3, (LT) 3 times; rep from *, end k3, (LT) twice.
Row 12—(LT) twice, * k3, (LT) 3 times; rep from *, end k3, (LT) twice, k1.
Row 14—K1, LT, * k3, (LT) 3 times; rep from *.
Row 16—LT, * k3, (LT) 3 times; rep from *, end k1.
Row 18—K4, * (LT) 3 times, k3; rep from *, end last repeat k2.

Repeat Rows 1–18.

Twilled Stripe Pattern

Contributed by Suzanne Pryor, Wichita, Kansas

The slip-chain technique is used here to make a simple and beautiful ribbed fabric. It is particularly interesting when left unpressed, so that the ribs are allowed to close up together.

Twilled Stripe Pattern

Multiple of 7 sts plus 2.

NOTE: Left Twist (LT) as follows: skip 1 st and knit the second st in *back* loop, then slip the skipped st purlwise onto right-hand needle, then slip the knit st also.

Row 1 (Wrong side) and all other wrong-side rows—K2, * p5, k2; rep from *.
Row 2—P2, * LT, k3, p2; rep from *.
Row 4—P2, * k1, LT, k2, p2; rep from *.
Row 6—P2, * k2, LT, k1, p2; rep from *.
Row 8—P2, * k3, LT, p2; rep from *.

Repeat Rows 1–8.

111

Pier-Glass Pattern

Pier-Glass Pattern

Here is an attractive fancy-rib design for sweaters; its elements are simple, but its overall effect is very nice. Work it with smallish needles so that the twists, when purled on the right side, will not show too many or too large openings in the fabric.

Multiple of 13 sts plus 1.

Rows 1 and 3 (Wrong side)—P2, * k2, p1, k4, p1, k2, p3; rep from *, end last repeat p2.

Row 2—K2, * p2, k1, p4, k1, p2, k3; rep from *, end last repeat k2.

Row 4—K2, * p2, LT, p2, RT, p2, k3; rep from *, end last repeat k2.

Row 5—P2, * k3, p1, k2, p1, k3, p3; rep from *, end last repeat p2.

Row 6—K1, * LT, p2, LT, RT, p2, RT, k1; rep from *.

Row 7—P1, * k1, p1, k3, p2, k3, p1, k1, p1; rep from *.

Row 8—K1, * p1, LT, (p2, RT) twice, p1, k1; rep from *.

Row 9—P1, * k2, p1, k6, p1, k2, p1; rep from *.

Row 10—K1, * p2, LT, p4, RT, p2, k1; rep from *.

Rows 11 and 13—P1, * k3, p1, k4, p1, k3, p1; rep from *.

Row 12—K1, * p3, k1, p4, k1, p3, k1; rep from *.

Row 14—K1, * p2, RT, p4, LT, p2, k1; rep from *.

Row 15—P1, * k2, p1, k2, p2, (k2, p1) twice; rep from *.

Row 16—K1, * p1, (RT, p2) twice, LT, p1, k1; rep from *.

Rows 17 and 19—Repeat Rows 7 and 5.

Row 18—K1, * RT, p2, RT, LT, p2, LT, k1; rep from *.

Row 20—K2, * p2, RT, p2, LT, p2, k3; rep from *, end last repeat k2.

Repeat Rows 1–20.

Brocade Chevron

Brocade Chevron

Here is a beautiful pattern for sports wear, coats, yokes, or borders. The chevrons are done in Seed Stitch and set off by twisted edges. The fabric is firm and dense, and is best worked on smallish needles so that the stitches will lie close.

Multiple of 10 sts plus 4.

NOTES: Right Twist (RT)—skip 1 st and knit the 2nd st, then knit the skipped st, then sl both sts from needle together.

Left Twist (LT)—skip 1 st and knit the 2nd st in *back* loop, then knit the skipped st in *front* loop, then sl both sts from needle together.

All sl-sts are slipped with yarn in *front* (wrong side of fabric).

Row 1 (Wrong side)—Purl.
Row 2—K1, * RT, k8; rep from *, end RT, k1.
Row 3—P1, * sl 2, p8; rep from *, end sl 2, p1.
Row 4—K2, * LT, k6, RT; rep from *, end k2.
Row 5—K1, p1, * k1, sl 1, p6, sl 1, p1; rep from *, end k1, p1.
Row 6—P1, k1, * p1, LT, k4, RT, k1; rep from *, end p1, k1.
Row 7—(K1, p1) twice, * sl 1, p4, sl 1, (k1, p1) twice; rep from *.
Row 8—(P1, k1) twice, * LT, k2, RT, (p1, k1) twice; rep from *.
Row 9—K1, * (p1, k1) twice, sl 1, p2, sl 1, p1, k1; rep from *, end p1, k1, p1.
Row 10—P1, * (k1, p1) twice, LT, RT, k1, p1; rep from *, end k1, p1, k1.
Row 11—* (K1, p1) 3 times, sl 2, k1, p1; rep from *, end (k1, p1) twice.
Row 12—* (P1, k1) 3 times, RT, p1, k1; rep from *, end (p1, k1) twice.
Row 13—* K1, p1; rep from *.
Row 14—P1, * RT, (k1, p1) 4 times; rep from *, end RT, k1.
Row 15—K1, * sl 2, (p1, k1) 4 times; rep from *, end sl 2, k1.
Row 16—K2, * LT, (p1, k1) 3 times, RT; rep from *, end k2.
Row 17—P3, * sl 1, (k1, p1) 3 times, sl 1, p2; rep from *, end p1.
Row 18—K3, * LT, (k1, p1) twice, RT, k2; rep from *, end k1.
Row 19—P4, * sl 1, (p1, k1) twice, sl 1, p4; rep from *.
Row 20—K4, * LT, p1, k1, RT, k4; rep from *.
Row 21—P5, * sl 1, k1, p1, sl 1, p6; rep from *, end last repeat p5.
Row 22—K5, * LT, RT, k6; rep from *, end last repeat k5.
Row 23—P6, * sl 2, p8; rep from *, end last repeat p6.
Row 24—K6, * RT, k8; rep from *, end last repeat k6.

Repeat Rows 1–24.

Knit-Twist Lattice

This pattern makes a fine, sharp, clean lattice design on a knit-stitch ground. A single panel of 18 stitches is beautiful in fancy sweaters.

Multiple of 16 sts plus 2.

Row 1 (Wrong side) and all other wrong-side rows—Purl.
Row 2—K1, * LT, k4, RT; rep from *, end k1.
Row 4—K2, * LT, k2, RT, k2; rep from *.
Row 6—K3, * LT, RT, k4; rep from *, end last repeat k3.
Row 8—K4, * RT, k6; rep from *, end last repeat k4.
Row 10—K3, * RT, LT, k4; rep from *, end last repeat k3.
Row 12—K2, * RT, k2, LT, k2; rep from *.
Row 14—K1, * RT, k4, LT; rep from *, end k1.
Row 16—K8, * LT, k6; rep from *, end k2.

Repeat Rows 1–16.

Knit Twist Lattice

113

Fractured Lattice

Fractured Lattice

This pattern is simple to work and fascinating to look at. The twist-stitch lattice is broken, here, into overlapping chevrons made by diagonal lines. The herringbone effect makes it a good pattern for coats and suits.

Multiple of 8 sts.

Row 1 (Wrong side) and all other wrong-side rows—Purl.
Row 2—* LT, k2, LT, RT; rep from *.
Row 4—K1, * LT, k2, RT, k2; rep from *, end last repeat k1.
Row 6—* RT, LT, RT, k2; rep from *.
Row 8—K3, * LT, k2, RT, k2; rep from *, end LT, k3.

Repeat Rows 1–8.

Carved Diamond Pattern

Carved Diamond Pattern

Multiple of 16 sts plus 1.

Row 1 (Wrong side) and all other wrong-side rows—Purl.
Row 2—K1, * (LT) 3 times, k3, (RT) 3 times, k1; rep from *.
Row 4—K2, * (LT) 3 times, k1, (RT) 3 times, k3; rep from *, end last repeat k2.
Rows 6 and 8—Repeat Rows 2 and 4.
Row 10—Knit.
Row 12—K2, * (RT) 3 times, k1, (LT) 3 times, k3; rep from *, end last repeat k2.
Row 14—K1, * (RT) 3 times, k3, (LT) 3 times, k1; rep from *.
Rows 16 and 18—Repeat Rows 12 and 14.
Row 20—Knit.

Repeat Rows 1–20.

Heraldic Pattern

Crossed swords and battle-flags hanging on a rough stone wall—does this design suggest such things to you? Even if it doesn't, it is still an exceedingly handsome pattern for a man's or a boy's sweater, and so easy to work that you can use it all over a garment for a *big* man whose sweaters take a lot of knitting.

Multiple of 12 sts.

Rows 1, 3, 5, and 7 (Wrong side)—K2, * p2, k4; rep from *, end p2, k2.
Row 2—K2, * RT, k4, LT, k4; rep from *, end last repeat k2.
Row 4—Knit.

Row 6—Repeat Row 2.
Row 8—K3, * LT, k2, RT, k6; rep from *, end last repeat k3.
Row 9—K2, * p3, k2, p3, k4; rep from *, end last repeat k2.
Row 10—K4, * LT, RT, k8; rep from *, end last repeat k4.
Row 11—K2, * p8, k4; rep from *, end last repeat k2.
Row 12—K5, * RT, k10; rep from *, end last repeat k5.
Rows 13 and 15—Repeat Rows 11 and 9.
Row 14—K4, * RT, LT, k8, rep from *, end last repeat k4.
Row 16—K3, * RT, k2, LT, k6; rep from *, end last repeat k3.
Rows 17, 19, 21, and 23—Repeat Rows 1, 3, 5, and 7.
Row 18—K2, * LT, k4, RT, k4; rep from *, end last repeat k2.
Row 20—Knit.
Row 22—Repeat Row 18.
Row 24—K9, rep from * of Row 8; end k3.
Row 25—K2, p2, * k4, p3, k2, p3; rep from *, end k4, p2, k2.
Row 26—K10, rep from * of Row 10; end k2.
Row 27—K2, p2, * k4, p8; rep from *, end k4, p2, k2.
Row 28—K11, * LT, k10; rep from *, end k1.
Rows 29 and 31—Repeat Rows 27 and 25.
Row 30—K10, rep from * of Row 14; end k2.
Row 32—K9, rep from * of Row 16; end k3.

Repeat Rows 1–32.

Heraldic Pattern

Ribbed Leaf Pattern

This beautiful twisted-all-over fabric is reminiscent of the shapes of fossilized fern leaves traced in rock. A single motif can be worked in cable fashion, see Ribbed Leaf Panel.

Multiple of 16 sts plus 1.

Row 1 (Wrong side) and all other wrong-side rows—Purl.
Row 2—K1, * LT, (RT) twice, k3, (LT) twice, RT, k1; rep from *.
Row 4—K2, * LT, (RT) twice, k1, (LT) twice, RT, k3; rep from *, end last repeat k2.
Row 6—K1, * (LT) twice, RT, k3, LT, (RT) twice, k1; rep from *.
Row 8—K2, * (LT) twice, RT, k1, LT, (RT) twice, k3; rep from *, end last repeat k2.
Row 10—K1, * (LT) 3 times, k3, (RT) 3 times, k1; rep from *.
Row 12—K2, * (LT) 3 times, k1, (RT) 3 times, k3; rep from *, end last repeat k2.
Rows 14, 16, 18, 20, and 22—Repeat Rows 10, 8, 6, 4, and 2.
Row 24—K2, * (RT) 3 times, k1, (LT) 3 times, k3; rep from *, end last repeat k2.
Row 26—K1, * (RT) 3 times, k3, (LT) 3 times, k1; rep from *.
Row 28—Repeat Row 24.

Repeat Rows 1–28.

Ribbed Leaf Pattern

115

Double Lattice

Double Lattice

Here is a pattern that will give the knitter plenty of practice in the use of twist stitches, since nearly all of them are twisted on the right-side rows. It also demonstrates how the twist-stitch technique can be a time-saver; imagine how long this handsome fabric would take to make, if all the stitches were cabled instead of twisted!

Multiple of 6 sts plus 4.

Row 1 (Wrong side) and all other wrong-side rows—Purl.
Row 2— * LT, (RT) twice; rep from *, end LT, RT.
Row 4—K1, LT, * RT, (LT) twice; rep from *, end k1.
Row 6—(LT) twice, * k2, (LT) twice; rep from *.
Row 8—K1, * (LT) twice, RT; rep from *, end LT, k1.
Row 10—RT, * LT, (RT) twice; rep from *, end LT.
Row 12—K3, * (RT) twice, k2; rep from *, end k1.

Repeat Rows 1–12.

Three Twist Patterns with Openwork: Diagonal Crepe Stitch, Deep Waffle Pattern, and Wide Waffle Pattern

All three of these patterns are deep in texture, thick but light and fluffy. Diagonal Crepe Stitch is a good thermal fabric; try it in a pair of "longjohns"! (Very handsome ones they will be, too.) Deep Waffle Pattern comes from Switzerland, and in fine yarn makes a delicate and lovely sweater or shell. Wide Waffle Pattern is an enlarged version with the pattern lines slanted more toward the horizontal.

I. DIAGONAL CREPE STITCH

Multiple of 4 sts plus 3.

Row 1 (Right side)—P1, RT, * p2, RT; rep from *.
Row 2—K1, * yo, p2 tog, k2; rep from *, end yo, p2 tog.
Row 3—K1, * p2, RT; rep from *, end p2.
Row 4—K3, * yo, p2 tog, k2; rep from *.

Repeat Rows 1–4.

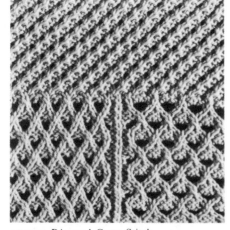

ABOVE: *Diagonal Crepe Stitch*
BELOW, LEFT: *Deep Waffle Pattern*
BELOW, RIGHT: *Wide Waffle Pattern*

II. DEEP WAFFLE PATTERN

Multiple of 4 sts plus 2.

Row 1 (Right side)—P2, * RT, p2; rep from *.
Row 2—K2, * p2, k2; rep from *.
Row 3—P1, * k2 tog, (yo) twice, ssk; rep from *, end p1.
Row 4—P2, * (k1, p1) into the double yo of previous row, p2; rep from *.
Row 5—K2, * p2, LT; rep from *, end p2, k2.
Row 6—P2, * k2, p2; rep from *.
Row 7—P1, yo, * ssk, k2 tog, (yo) twice; rep from *, end ssk, k2 tog, yo, p1.
Row 8—K2, * p2, (k1, p1) into the double yo of previous row; rep from *, end p2, k2.

Repeat Rows 1–8

III. WIDE WAFFLE PATTERN

Multiple of 6 sts plus 4.

Row 1 (Right side)—K2, p2, * LT, p4; rep from *, end LT, p2, k2.
Row 2—K4, * p2, k4; rep from *.
Row 3—K2, * k3 tog, yo, sl 1—k2 tog—psso; rep from *, end k2.
Row 4—K2, p1, * (k1, p1) twice in the yo of previous row, p2; rep from *, end last repeat p1, k2 instead of p2.
Row 5—K3, * p4, RT; rep from *, end p4, k3.
Row 6—K2, p1, * k4, p2; rep from *, end k4, p1, k2.
Row 7—K2, yo, * sl 1—k2 tog—psso, k3 tog, yo; rep from *, end k2.
Row 8—K2, (k1, p1) into the yo, * p2, (k1, p1) twice in the yo of previous row; rep from *, end p2, (k1, p1) into the yo, k2.

Repeat Rows 1–8.

Knit-Twist Lattice with Lace

This fabric looks beautiful and very fancy, although it is not at all difficult to work. *Notice* that in Rows 4 and 28 there is a double yo in the middle of each motif, although in the directions this double yo is split into two different sets of parentheses. Also, *notice* that another double yo is formed by the last and the first directions of Rows 10, 14, 18, and 22, when these pattern rows are repeated across. Always bear in mind that each double yo makes two new stitches on the needle, and is always worked (k1, p1) on the return row.

Multiple of 14 sts plus 2.

Row 1 (Wrong side) and all other wrong-side rows—Purl, working (k1, p1) into every double yo from a previous row.
Row 2—K4, * (yo, ssk) twice, (k2 tog, yo) twice, k2, RT, k2; rep from *, end last repeat k4 instead of k2, RT, k2.

Knit-Twist Lattice With Lace

117

Row 4—K1, * LT, k1, (k2 tog, yo) twice, (yo, ssk) twice, k1, RT; rep from *, end k1.
Row 6—K1, * k1, LT, k2, yo, ssk, k2 tog, yo, k2, RT, k1; rep from *, end k1.
Row 8—K1, * k2, LT, k1, k2 tog, (yo) twice, ssk, k1, RT, k2; rep from *, end k1.
Row 10—K1, * yo, ssk, k1, LT, k4, RT, k1, k2 tog, yo; rep from *, end k1.
Row 12—K1, * k2 tog, yo, k2, LT, k2, RT, k2, yo, ssk; rep from *, end k1.
Row 14—K1, * (yo, ssk) twice, k1, LT, RT, k1, (k2 tog, yo) twice; rep from *, end k1.
Row 16—K1, * (k2 tog, yo) twice, k2, LT, k2, (yo, ssk) twice; rep from *, end k1.
Row 18—K1, * (yo, ssk) twice, k1, RT, LT, k1, (k2 tog, yo) twice; rep from *, end k1.
Row 20—K1, * k2 tog, yo, k2, RT, k2, LT, k2, yo, ssk; rep from *, end k1.
Row 22—K1, * yo, ssk, k1, RT, k4, LT, k1, k2 tog, yo; rep from *, end k1.
Row 24—K3, * RT, k1, k2 tog, (yo) twice, ssk, k1, LT, k4; rep from *, end last repeat k3 instead of k4.
Row 26—K2, * RT, k2, yo, ssk, k2 tog, yo, k2, LT, k2; rep from *.
Row 28—K1, * RT, k1, (k2 tog, yo) twice, (yo, ssk) twice, k1, LT; rep from *, end k1.

Repeat Rows 1-28.

Gable Pattern

Gable Pattern

Little "windows" of faggoting add interest, here, to an allover pattern of twist-stitch chevrons. Notice that the decreases on either side of the openwork are worked in opposition to the slant of the stitches, to make sharp clear edges.

Multiple of 10 sts plus 2.

Row 1 (Right side)—K4, * RT, LT, k1, ssk, yo, k3; rep from *, end last repeat k1.
Row 2—P9, * p2 tog, yo, p8; rep from *, end p2 tog, yo, p1.
Row 3—K3, * RT, k2, LT, k4; rep from *, end last repeat k3.
Row 4—Purl.
Row 5—K2, * RT, k4, LT, k2; rep from *.
Row 6—P4, * p2 tog, yo, p8; rep from *, end p2 tog, yo, p6.
Row 7—K1, * RT, k1, ssk, yo, k3, LT; rep from *, end k1.
Rows 8, 10, 12, and 14—K2, * p2, p2 tog, yo, p4, k2; rep from *.
Rows 9, 11, and 13—P2, * k2, ssk, yo, k4, p2; rep from *.
Row 15—K1, * LT, k1, ssk, yo, k3, RT; rep from *, end k1.
Rows 16, 18, and 20—Repeat Rows 6, 4, and 2.
Row 17—K2, * LT, k4, RT, k2; rep from *.
Row 19—K3, * LT, k2, RT, k4; rep from *, end last repeat k3.
Row 21—K4, * LT, RT, k1, ssk, yo, k3; rep from *, end last repeat k1.
Rows 22, 24, 26, and 28—P5, * k2, p2, p2 tog, yo, p4; rep from *, end last repeat p1.
Rows 23, 25, and 27—K5, * p2, k2, ssk, yo, k4; rep from *, end last repeat k1.

Repeat Rows 1-28.

118

Three Knit-Twist Panels: V, Tent, and Heart

These are three fairly wide cable substitutes, all using the knit-twist method of crossing stitches. I and II, the "V" and the "Tent", are quite straightforward. Either could be used in a ribbed or panel-patterned skirt, as a minor design in a fisherman sweater, or as an allover pattern on a multiple of 12 stitches plus 2. These twisted diagonal stitches could also be arranged as zigzags, diamonds, braids, or plain diagonals running all to the right or all to the left—as when I or II is cut in half to make a panel 5 stitches wide with only the first or second half of each pattern rows being worked.

The "Heart" motif (III) is not often seen in knitting patterns, for the good reason that knitting, by its very nature, makes it difficult to form a rounded top to a design. The upper curves of any heart-shaped pattern, therefore, are usually made in some rather awkward way, by working 4 or 5 stitches together, for instance. This third panel suffers from the customary awkwardness but does manage to achieve a recognizable heart shape.

Knit-Twist Panels
LEFT: *"V" Panel*
CENTER: *Tent Panel*
RIGHT: *Heart Panel*

Each pattern: Panel of 14 sts.

Each pattern Row 1 (Wrong side) and every other wrong-side row—K2, p10, k2.

I. "V" PANEL

Row 2—P2, k3, RT, LT, k3, p2.
Row 4—P2, k2, RT, k2, LT, k2, p2.
Row 6—P2, k1, RT, k4, LT, k1, p2.
Row 8—P2, RT, k6, LT, p2.

Repeat Rows 1–8.

II. TENT PANEL

Row 2—P2, LT, k6, RT, p2.
Row 4—P2, k1, LT, k4, RT, k1, p2.
Row 6—P2, k2, LT, k2, RT, k2, p2.
Row 8—P2, k3, LT, RT, k3, p2.
Row 10—P2, k4, RT, k4, p2.

Repeat Rows 1–10.

119

III. HEART PANEL

Rows 2, 4, 6, and 8—Repeat Rows 2, 4, 6, and 8 of Pattern I.
Row 10—Repeat Row 2 again.
Row 12—P2, LT, RT, k2, LT, RT, p2.
Row 14—P2, k1, M1, k2 tog-b, k4, k2 tog, M1, k1, p2.
Row 16—P2, k10, p2.

Repeat Rows 1–16.

Tent Cable

CENTER PANEL: *Tent Cable*
SIDE PANELS: *Pigtail*

Repeated on a multiple of 14 sts instead of in a single panel, this pattern makes an attractive chevron.

Panel of 14 sts.

Row 1 (Right side)—(LT) twice, p6, (RT) twice.
Row 2—K1, p3, k6, p3, k1.
Row 3—P1, (LT) twice, p4, (RT) twice, p1.
Row 4—K2, p3, k4, p3, k2.
Row 5—P2, (LT) twice, p2, (RT) twice, p2.
Row 6—K3, p3, k2, p3, k3.
Row 7—P3, (LT) twice, (RT) twice, p3.
Row 8—K4, p6, k4.
Row 9—P4, LT, k2, RT, p4.
Row 10—K5, p4, k5.
Row 11—P5, LT, RT, p5.
Row 12—P3, k3, p2, k3, p3.

Repeat Rows 1–12.

Pigtail

Here is a very attractive small braided rib, which can be used as a single cable panel or worked as a fancy ribbing on a multiple of 5 stitches plus 2. When left unpressed, the Pigtail is very highly embossed, rounded and springy.

Panel of 7 sts.

Rows 1 and 3 (Wrong side)—K2, p3, k2.
Row 2—P2, RT, k1, p2.
Row 4—P2, k1, LT, p2.

Repeat Rows 1–4.

120

Twist-Rib Chevron

The outlines of this design happen to be filled in with twisted ribs—this is traditional—but they could be filled in with garter stitch, seed stitch, moss stitch, or plain stockinette. With any "filling" you like, this is a beautiful pattern for fancy sweaters, afghans, or dresses.

Panel of 18 sts.

Row 1 (Wrong side) K2, p1-b, k1, p1, k3, p2, k3, p1, k1, p1-b, k2.
Row 2 P2, k1-b, (RT, p3) twice, LT, k1-b, p2.
Row 3—K2, p2, (k4, p2) twice, k2.
Row 4—P2, RT, p3, RT, LT, p3, LT, p2.
Row 5—K7, p4, k7.
Row 6—P6, RT, k2-b, LT, p6.
Row 7—K6, p1, k1, p2-b, k1, p1, k6.
Row 8—P5, RT, p1, k2-b, p1, LT, p5.
Row 9—K5, p2, k1, p2-b, k1, p2, k5.
Row 10—P4, RT, k1-b, p1, k2-b, p1, k1-b, LT, p4.
Row 11—K4, p1, k1, p1-b, k1, p2-b, k1, p1-b, k1, p1, k4.
Row 12—P3, RT, p1, k1-b, p1, k2 b, p1, k1-b, p1, LT, p3.
Row 13—K3, (p2, k1, p1-b, k1) twice, p2, k3.
Row 14—P2, RT, k1-b, p1, k1-b, RT, LT, k1-b, p1, k1-b, LT, p2.
Row 15—K2, p1, k1, p1-b, k1, p6, k1, p1-b, k1, p1, k2.
Row 16—P2, (k1-b, p1) twice, RT, k2, LT, (p1, k1-b) twice, p2.
Row 17—K2, (p1-b, k1) twice, p1, k1, p2, k1, p1, (k1, p1-b) twice, k2.
Row 18—P2, k1-b, p1, k1-b, (RT, p1) twice, LT, k1-b, p1, k1-b, p2.
Row 19—K2, p1-b, k1, (p2, k2) twice, p2, k1, p1-b, k2.
Row 20—P2, k1-b, p1, RT, p2, k2, p2, LT, p1, k1-b, p2.

Repeat Rows 1–20.

CENTER PANEL: *Twist-Rib Chevron*
SIDE PANELS: *Rapunzel's Braid*

Rapunzel's Braid

Try this beautiful little braid panel on each side of a V neckline, or flanking a wide cable. To make two braids twist in opposite directions, begin one of them with Row 1 and the other with Row 5.

Panel of 10 sts.

Rows 1 and 3 (Wrong side)—K3, p5, k2.
Row 2—P2, k3, RT, p3.
Row 4—P2, LT, RT, LT, p2.
Rows 5 and 7—K2, p5, k3.
Row 6—P3, LT, k3, p2.
Row 8—P2, RT, LT, RT, p2.

Repeat Rows 1–8.

Briar Rose

LEFT: *Briar Rose*
CENTER: *Teardrop Pendant on Seed Stitch*
RIGHT: *Square Knot*

"Briar stems" gracefully entwined, and bobble-like "rosebuds", make this an exceptionally pretty panel to combine with lace, as well as with other twist patterns and with cables.

Panel of 13 sts.

Row 1 (Wrong side)—K3, p1, k1, p2, k2, p1, k3.
Row 2—P3, LT, p1, LT, RT, p3.
Row 3—K4, p2, k2, p1, k4.
Row 4—P2, (k1, yo, k1) in next st, turn and p3, turn and k3 wrapping yarn twice for each knit st; p1, LT, p1, RT, p4.
Row 5—K4, p2, k1, p1, k2, sl next 3 sts dropping extra wraps, sl the same 3 sts back to left-hand needle and p3 tog-b; k2.
Row 6—P2, LT, p1, k1-b, RT, LT, p3.
Row 7—K3, p1, k2, p2, k1, p1, k3.
Row 8—P3, LT, RT, p1, RT, p3.
Row 9—K4, p1, k2, p2, k4.
Row 10—P4, LT, p1, RT, p1, (k1, yo, k1) in next st, turn and p3, turn and k3 wrapping yarn twice for each knit st; p2.
Row 11—K2, sl next 3 sts dropping extra wraps, sl the same 3 sts back to left-hand needle and p3 tog; k2, p1, k1, p2, k4.
Row 12—P3, RT, LT, k1-b, p1, RT, p2.

Repeat Rows 1–12.

Teardrop Pendant on Seed Stitch

Panel of 19 sts.

NOTES: Increase Right (inc R)—Insert right-hand needle downward into the *back* of the st *in the row below* the next st on left-hand needle (i.e., into the purled head of st on the back of the fabric), and knit; then knit the st on left-hand needle in the usual way.

Increase Left (inc L)—Knit (from front) into the st *in the row below* the next st on left-hand needle; then knit the st on left-hand needle in the usual way.

Row 1 (Wrong side)—K6, (p1, k1) 3 times, p1, k6.
Row 2—P5, RT, (k1, p1) twice, k1, LT, p5.
Row 3—K5, p2, (k1, p1) 3 times, p1, k5.
Row 4—P4, RT, (p1, k1) 3 times, p1, LT, p4.
Row 5—K4, (p1, k1) 5 times, p1, k4.
Row 6—P3, RT, (k1, p1) twice, (k1, p1, k1) in next st, (p1, k1) twice, LT, p3.

Row 7—K3, p2, k1, p1, k1, p5, k1, p1, k1, p2, k3.
Row 8—P2, RT, (p1, k1) twice, p1, inc R, k1, inc L, p1, (k1, p1) twice, LT, p2.
Row 9—K2, (p1, k1) 3 times, p7, (k1, p1) 3 times, k2.
Row 10—P2, k1-b, (k1, p1) 3 times, inc R, k3, inc L, (p1, k1) 3 times, k1-b, p2.
Row 11—K2, (p1, k1) 3 times, p9, (k1, p1) 3 times, k2.
Row 12—P2, k1-b, (k1, p1) 3 times, k2, sl 2—k1—p2sso, k2, (p1, k1) 3 times, k1-b, p2.
Row 13—Repeat Row 9.
Row 14—P2, k1-b, (k1, p1) 3 times, k1, sl 2—k1—p2sso, k1, (p1, k1) 3 times, k1-b, p2.
Row 15—K2, (p1, k1) 3 times, p5, (k1, p1) 3 times, k2.
Row 16—P2, k1-b, (k1, p1) 3 times, sl 2—k1—p2sso, (p1, k1) 3 times, k1-b, p2.
Row 17—K2, (p1, k1) 3 times, p3, (k1, p1) 3 times, k2.
Row 18—P2, LT, p1, k1, p1, RT, k1, LT, p1, k1, p1, RT, p2.
Row 19—K3, p2, k1, (p3, k1) twice, p2, k3.
Row 20—P3, LT, k1, RT, p1, k1, p1, LT, k1, RT, p3.

Repeat Rows 1–20.

Square Knot

The knit stitches in this simple panel follow exactly the course taken by the strands in an ordinary square knot. The pattern is excellent for sportswear of all kinds.

Panel of 12 sts.

Rows 1 and 3 (Wrong side)—K2, p1, k6, p1, k2.
Rows 2 and 4—P2, k1-b, p6, k1-b, p2.
Rows 5 and 7—K2, p1, k2, p2, k2, p1, k2.
Row 6—P2, k1-b, p2, RT, p2, k1-b, p2.
Row 8—P2, (LT, RT) twice, p2.
Rows 9 and 11—K3, p2, k2, p2, k3.
Row 10—P3, RT, p2, LT, p3.
Row 12—P3, k2, p2, k2, p3.
Rows 13 through 19—Repeat Rows 9 through 12, then Rows 9 through 11 again.
Row 20—P2, (RT, LT) twice, p2.
Rows 21 and 22—Repeat Rows 5 and 6.
Rows 23 through 26—Repeat Rows 1 through 4.

Repeat Rows 1–26.

Ribbed Leaf Panel

CENTER PANEL: *Ribbed Leaf Panel*
SIDE PANELS: *Grapevine Twist*

Panel of 19 sts.

Row 1 (Wrong side)—K8, p3, k8.
Row 2—P7, RT, k1, LT, p7.
Row 3—K7, p5, k7.
Row 4—P6, RT, k3, LT, p6.
Row 5—K6, p7, k6.
Row 6—P5, (RT) twice, k1, (LT) twice, p5.
Row 7—K5, p9, k5.
Row 8—P4, (RT) twice, k3, (LT) twice, p4.
Row 9—K4, p11, k4.
Row 10—P3, (RT) 3 times, k1, (LT) 3 times, p3.
Row 11—K3, p13, k3.
Row 12—P2, (RT) 3 times, k3, (LT) 3 times, p2.
Row 13—K2, p15, k2.
Row 14—P2, k1, (RT) 3 times, k1, (LT) 3 times, k1, p2.
Rows 15, 17, 19, 21, 23, and 25—Repeat Rows 13, 11, 9, 7, 5, and 3.
Row 16—P2, LT, (RT) twice, k3, (LT) twice, RT, p2.
Row 18—P3, LT, (RT) twice, k1, (LT) twice, RT, p3.
Row 20—P4, LT, RT, k3, LT, RT, p4.
Row 22—P5, LT, RT, k1, LT, RT, p5.
Row 24—P6, LT, k3, RT, p6.
Row 26—P7, LT, k1, RT, p7.

Repeat Rows 1–26.

Grapevine Twist

Panel of 13 sts.

NOTE: Make Bobble (MB) as follows—(k1, yo, k1, yo, k1) in one st, turn and k5, turn and p5, turn and k1, sl 1—k2 tog—psso, k1, turn and p3 tog, completing bobble.

Row 1 (Wrong side) and all other wrong-side rows—Purl.
Row 2—K2, LT, k2, RT, k5.
Row 4—K3, LT, RT, k6.
Row 6—K4, LT, k4, MB, k2.
Row 8—K5, LT, k2, RT, k2.
Row 10—K6, LT, RT, k3.
Row 12—K2, MB, k4, RT, k4.

Repeat Rows 1–12.

124

Sheepfold

Contributed by Elizabeth Zimmermann, Milwaukee, Wisconsin

This pattern was originally planned for circular knitting, so that all rows would be worked from the right side. To do it in this way, simply work all odd-numbered rows backward, substituting "knit" for "purl" and vice versa, and working plain RT and LT instead of RRT and RLT. When converted into back-and-forth knitting, the pattern calls for some twists made on the wrong side. (See Sunrise Shell Pattern for additional discussion of RLT.)

Notice that the usual right-side Left Twist is to be done by the classical method rather than the new method of working the two stitches together. The reason for this is that the two stitches together may become too tight for convenience in working the subsequent *wrong*-side twist. The Right Twist, on the other hand, can be worked either way (it is tidier when done by the new method) and so this is not described in the notes.

SIDE PANELS: *Sheepfold*
CENTER PANEL: *Medallion with Leaf*

Panel of 16 sts.

NOTES: Left Twist (LT)— skip 1 st and knit the 2nd st in *back* loop, then knit the skipped st in front loop in the usual way, and sl both sts from needle together.

Reverse Left Twist (RLT)—skip 1 st and purl the 2nd st in *back* loop, then purl the skipped st, then sl both sts from needle together.

Reverse Right Twist (RRT)—There are two methods of working this twist, the preferred one given first. (1) Skip 1 st and purl the 2nd st, then p2 tog (the skipped st and the 2nd st) and sl both sts from needle together. (2) Skip 1 st and purl the 2nd st, then purl the skipped st and sl both sts from needle together.

Row 1 (Wrong side)—K2, p12, k2.
Row 2—P2, LT, k8, RT, p2.
Row 3—K3, RRT, p6, RLT, p1, k2.
Row 4—P2, k2, LT, k4, RT, p4.
Row 5—K5, RRT, p2, RLT, p3, k2.
Row 6—P2, k4, LT, RT, p6.
Row 7—K7, RLT, p5, k2.
Row 8—P2, k6, LT, p6.
Row 9—K5, RLT, p7, k2.
Row 10—P2, k8, LT, p4.
Row 11—K3, RLT, p9, k2.
Row 12—P2, k10, LT, p2.
Rows 13 and 14—Repeat Rows 1 and 2.
Row 15—K2, p1, RRT, p6, RLT, k3.
Row 16—P4, LT, k4, RT, k2, p2.
Row 17—K2, p3, RRT, p2, RLT, k5.

125

Row 18—P6, LT, RT, k4, p2.
Row 19—K2, p5, RRT, k7.
Row 20—P6, RT, k6, p2.
Row 21—K2, p7, RRT, k5.
Row 22—P4, RT, k8, p2.
Row 23—K2, p9, RRT, k3.
Row 24—P2, RT, k10, p2.

Repeat Rows 1–24.

Medallion with Leaf

This pattern is attractive as a panel in fancy sweaters such as Aran knits. Or, it can be used to "dress up" afghans, coat sleeves, hats, mittens, or knee socks. There are, of course, many possible variations; the medallions can be larger or smaller, or filled in with purl, seed or moss stitch instead of garter stitch, or featuring some other motif instead of the embossed leaf in the center.

Panel of 19 sts.

NOTES: For RT and LT, RRT and RLT, see the Notes to Sheepfold.

Rows 1 and 3 (Wrong side)—K8, p3, k8.
Row 2—P8, skip 2 sts and knit into 3rd st, then into 1st and 2nd sts and sl all three together from needle (Twist 3); p8.
Row 4—P7, RT, k1-b, LT, p7.
Row 5—K6, RLT, k1, p1, k1, RRT, k6.
Row 6—P5, RT, k2, k1-b, k2, LT, p5.
Row 7—K5, (p1, k3) twice, p1, k5.
Row 8—P4, RT, k3, k1-b, k3, LT, p4.
Row 9—K4, (p1, k4) 3 times.
Row 10—P3, RT, k2, RT, k1-b, LT, k2, LT, p3.
Row 11—K3, p1, k2, RLT, k1, p1, k1, RRT, k2, p1, k3.
Row 12—P2, RT, k1, RT, p2, k1-b, p2, LT, k1, LT, p2.
Row 13—(K2, p1) twice, k3, p1, k3, (p1, k2) twice.
Row 14—P2, k4, p3, (k1, yo, k1, yo, k1) in next st, p3, k4, p2.
Rows 15 and 17—(K2, p1) twice, k3, p5, k3, (p1, k2) twice.
Row 16—P2, k4, p3, k5, p3, k4, p2.
Row 18—P2, k4, p3, ssk, k1, k2 tog, p3, k4, p2.
Row 19—(K2, p1) twice, k3, p3, k3, (p1, k2) twice.
Row 20—P2, k3, LT, p2, sl 1—k2 tog—psso, p2, RT, k3, p2.
Row 21—K2, p1, k3, p1, k5, p1, k3, p1, k2.
Row 22—P2, LT, k2, LT, p3, RT, k2, RT, p2.
Row 23—K3, (p1, k3) 4 times.
Row 24—P3, LT, k2, LT, p1, RT, k2, RT, p3.
Row 25—K4, p1, k3, p1, k1, p1, k3, p1, k4.

Row 26—P4, LT, k2, Twist 3, k2, RT, p4.
Row 27—K5, p1, k7, p1, k5.
Row 28—P5, LT, k5, RT, p5.
Row 29—K6, RRT, k3, RLT, k6.
Row 30—P7, LT, k1, RT, p7.

Repeat Rows 1–30.

Club Pattern

Here is a delightful combination of twists and bobbles, appropriate for all kinds of sportswear. Use it along with cables and other texture patterns.

Panel of 15 sts.

Row 1 (Wrong side)—K4, (p1, k1) 4 times, k3.
Row 2—P3, (RT) twice, p1, (LT) twice, p3.
Row 3—K3, (p1, k1) twice, k2, (p1, k1) twice, k2.
Row 4—P2, (RT) twice, p3, (LT) twice, p2.
Row 5—K2, (p1, k1) twice, k4, (p1, k1) twice, k1.
Row 6—P1, (RT) twice, p5, (LT) twice, p1.
Row 7—(K1, p1) twice, k7, (p1, k1) twice.
Row 8—P1, Make Bobble (MB) as follows: (k1, yo, k1, yo, k1) in next st, turn and p5, turn and ssk, k3 tog, pass ssk st over the k3-tog st, completing Bobble; p1, LT, p5, RT, p1, MB, p1.
Row 9—K4, p1, k5, p1, k4.
Row 10—P4, LT, p3, RT, p4.
Row 11—K5, p1, k3, p1, k5.
Row 12—P5, MB, p3, MB, p5.

Repeat Rows 1–12.

CENTER PANEL: *Club Pattern*
LEFT SIDE PANEL: *Right-Twist Ramp Pattern*
RIGHT SIDE PANEL: *Left-Twist Ramp Pattern*

Ramp Pattern

This design can slant upwards to the left or to the right, depending on how the knitter wishes to arrange it. Both versions are given. They can be worked separately, or placed together in combination.

Panel of 13 sts.

I. LEFT-TWIST RAMP PATTERN

Row 1 (Wrong side)—K1, (p1, k1) 6 times.
Row 2—P1, (LT) 3 times, p6.
Row 3—K6, (p1, k1) 3 times, k1.
Row 4—P2, (LT) 3 times, p2, Make Bobble (MB) as follows: (k1, yo, k1, yo, k1) in next st, turn and p5, turn and k5, then pass the 4th, 3rd, 2nd and 1st of these 5 sts separately over the last st made, completing Bobble; p2.
Row 5—K5, (p1, k1) 3 times, k2.
Row 6—P3, (LT) 3 times, p4.
Row 7—K4, (p1, k1) 3 times, k3.
Row 8—P4, (LT) 3 times, p3.
Row 9—K3, (p1, k1) 3 times, k4.
Row 10—P2, MB, p2, (LT) 3 times, p2.
Row 11—K2, (p1, k1) 3 times, k5.
Row 12—P6, (LT) 3 times, p1.

Repeat Rows 1–12.

II. RIGHT-TWIST RAMP PATTERN

Row 1 (Wrong side)—K1, (p1, k1) 6 times.
Row 2—P6, (RT) 3 times, p1.
Row 3—K2, (p1, k1) 3 times, k5.
Row 4—P2, MB in next st same as above, p2, (RT) 3 times, p2.
Row 5—K3, (p1, k1) 3 times, k4.
Row 6—P4, (RT) 3 times, p3.
Row 7—K4, (p1, k1) 3 times, k3.
Row 8—P3, (RT) 3 times, p4.
Row 9—K5, (p1, k1) 3 times, k2.
Row 10—P2, (RT) 3 times, p2, MB, p2.
Row 11—K6, (p1, k1) 3 times, k1.
Row 12—P1, (RT) 3 times, p6.

Repeat Rows 1–12.